American Country Churches

MUSEUM

American Country Churches

William Morgan

PHOTOGRAPHY BY

Radek Kurzaj

HARRY N. ABRAMS PUBLISHERS, INC. NEW YORK

American Country Churches Table of Contents

8

American Country Churches
by William Morgan

102

Coeur d'Alene Mission of the Sacred Heart

Cataldo, Idaho

CATHOLIC, 1846

126

Rehoboth Church

Union, West Virginia

METHODIST, 1786

148

Saint Wenceslaus Church

Spillville, Iowa

CATHOLIC, 1860

108

Telemarken Lutheran Church

Clark County, South Dakota

LUTHERAN, 1894

132

Star Island Meeting House

Isles of Shoals, New Hampshire

UNITARIAN, 1800

154

Assumption of the Blessed Virgin Mary Church

Rancho Barona, California

CATHOLIC, 1932

114

Saint Mary's Church

Emmorton, Maryland

EPISCOPAL, 1849

138

Yeocomico Church

Tucker Hill, Virginia

EPISCOPAL, 1706

158

Faith Chapel

Jekyll Island, Georgia

NONDENOMINATIONAL, 1904

120

Mission Espíritu Santo Church

Goliad, Texas

CATHOLIC, 1936

144

Antioch Baptist Church

Perry County, Alabama

BAPTIST, 2002

162

Bethabara Moravian Church

Winston-Salem, North Carolina

MORAVIAN, 1788

American Country Churches Table of Contents (continued)

for Carolyn
and in memory of Edward Myers
who preached at Phippsburg

ACKNOWLEDGMENTS

*M*any people contributed to *American County Churches*.

Stewards of all of these places—priests, pastors, ministers, historians, parishioners—shared their knowledge and enthusiasm, and opened their houses of worship to writer and photographer. History is cumulative, and this book depends heavily upon the generous assistance of state historic preservation officers across the United States, not to mention the scholars of American church architecture upon whose work we build—Peter Williams, Marilyn Chiat, and Dell Upton, to name just a few.

This project could not have been undertaken without exceptional research assistants, in this case, Whitney Morrill, Denise Dea, and especially Joseph Beach. Radek Kurzaj's images tell the story as well, if not better, than words can. Jayne Merkel connected me with Abrams editor Richard Olsen, who had the idea for this book. My wife Carolyn urged me to write *Country Churches*, and has been a contributor to the book throughout.

—WM

**BETHLEHEM NO. 2
MISSIONARY BAPTIST
CHURCH, SHAW, MISSISSIPPI**
This Bolivar County church is
typical of hundreds of small
African-American churches in
the Mississippi Delta, a region
known for cotton, the blues,
and churches.

American Country Churches

INTRODUCTION

The country church tells us who we are.

What we believe defines us, just as the churches we build symbolize our spiritual beliefs in physical form. As the most basic unit of civic architecture, churches also are landmarks of our history and signposts of our aspirations.

The country church—in a clearing, on the prairies, in the woods, along the shore—is one of the most enduring American images:

- *The white steeple awash in autumn colors on a calendar.*
- *A wedding party coming down the steps of a stone chapel in a society-page photo.*
- *A faded sepia glimpse of sodbusters formally lined up in their Sunday best before a simple frame church on the grasslands.*
- *An old postcard of Indian children posed before a mission.*
- *A Christmas card with a primitive painting showing sleighs and farm animals around a meetinghouse.*

These pictures are more than just memories. They are part of our national consciousness, for religion is one of the inescapable facts of American life. We are a nation of immigrants. And while millions of people came for economic opportunity, many of our forebears came here in search of religious freedom. Whether Jesuit or Puritan, the great impetus that first settled this land and laid the foundations of nationhood was religion. This is stating the obvious, perhaps, but it bears repeated telling.

The Pilgrims and the Puritans, for example, have a certain textbook quaintness today, like costumed figures in an historical tableau. Or worse, we recognize their theocracy as an intellectual dictatorship, more structured than the established church against which it rebelled. We may wish to forget that Quakers were hanged on Boston Common, not to mention the horrific events of the Salem witch trials. Such dark chapters were all-too-frequent fallout from attempts to create a religious society. But the reaction to such intolerance had some positive consequences.

The outspoken Puritan preacher Roger Williams was banished from Salem to Rhode Island. His new colony forbad an established church; the separation of church and state was so complete in Rhode Island that churches did not face the public common as elsewhere in New England. The colony on Narragansett Bay welcomed all faiths—Baptists, Quakers, Jews, and any kind of dissenters. Newport was the home of the first synagogue, and it was there that George Washington declared that our new country would not tolerate bigotry of any kind. Although set up as a haven for Quakers, Pennsylvania welcomed all faiths. Founder William Penn actively recruited German immigrants, while the Scotch-Irish, fleeing centuries of religious warfare, also found succor in Pennsylvania. The pattern set by visionaries like Williams and Penn opened the American colonies to Wesleyans and Moravians, Mennonites and Amish.

These seventeenth-century developments set the stage for even greater religious freedom. Still, thirteen colonies had a dozen different approaches to a state church. But with the coming of the War of Independence, the Deism, Unitarianism, and agnosticism of leaders such as Thomas Jefferson, Benjamin Franklin, and Thomas Paine fostered an official absence of religion that made it truly possible for people of all religious persuasions to feel free and safe. In declaring that all men were created equal, these Enlightenment gentlemen ignited a revolution that is still going on.

Despite the Founding Fathers' care to ensure all that ours would be a secular state, we are nonetheless a very religious country. The First Amendment to the Constitution notwithstanding, Americans feel almost duty bound to evoke the deity. The motto "In God We Trust" graces our currency, and we pledge allegiance to "one nation, under God." Many of our social and athletic events open with a prayer, while the denominational affiliation of candidates for public office is invariably of interest to the electorate. The words of our unofficial national hymn, "America the Beautiful," are accepted as completely appropriate: "God shed His grace on thee."

Maybe it is because we are all immigrants that we feel a special religious sense: it was so important to treasure and maintain at all costs that which we brought with us to an alien shore. Which leads to another irony, the melting pot. It would be impossible to have a representative sampling of all of America's various religious groups (there were about 1,500 sects here in the nineteenth century). But the recurrent theme of national identification that is so strong in many of these churches suggests that ethnicity was embraced rather than discarded.

There is no single American church—which is, of course, the whole point. Yet one might have expected assimilation to have occurred sooner and been more thorough. Think of the cities or towns where there are several Catholic churches—an Irish one, an Italian one, and maybe a French-Canadian, Polish, or Lithuanian one. Persecuted or not, people came here to worship unrestricted, and this invariably meant they worshiped as they had back in the place from whence they came. This was especially true in the countryside: some immigrant groups purposely chose a rural setting, hoping that it would be easier to maintain language and traditions in the country. Presumably, there would be less distraction, and none of the city evils that might corrupt youth.

An anti-urban bias was not a new phenomenon brought on by waves of newcomers in the 1800s. Part of America's

WEST PARISH MEETING HOUSE ("THE ROOSTER CHURCH"), WEST BARNSTABLE, MASSACHUSETTS
Even though early eighteenth century New England churches were not painted white, this 1717 Cape Cod structure exemplifies our ideal of the Colonial church.

appeal was its noncivilization, its closeness to nature, its connection with the land. To many of the early settlers, particularly Puritan divines, America was seen as uncorrupted—a second chance for the Old World, a new and unspoiled Eden as revealed after the Great Flood. The Founding Fathers' ideal society was agrarian. Thomas Jefferson's belief in an agricultural, non-European model determined the opening of the West through the Northwest Ordinance of 1785 and the Louisiana Purchase. The Manifest Destiny that took us to the Pacific shore was, in a word, ordained.

Americans have an almost inherent distrust of cities. And even though the Census of 1920 demonstrated that more of us were living in the city than in the country, we work constantly to reverse that, in a manner of speaking, by surrounding our urban cores with suburbs. The suburb is a domesticated wilderness: it is safe from all that is wild, while replicating the country and serving as substitute for it.

Americans believe themselves to be a country people, regardless of where we live. How else can we explain our continued faith in the landscape—our support of the Sierra Club and the Boy Scouts, the dream of a country place to which to retire, not to mention our love affair with cars tricked out for off-road exploration and trucks built for hauling livestock even if their knobby tires will never run on a dirt road. We share a deep-seated, unshakable belief that the country is redemptive.

Given that faith in the restorative power of nature, the country church is one of the places where we can touch base with our roots. There are, of course, equally important cultural indicators in city churches. But almost by definition, the country church implies having preserved the old ways and kept traditions alive, and its scale makes it easier for us to identify with. Often, too, the relative isolation of a rural area may mean that a church is less changed and thus perhaps closer to the original intentions of its builders. Having been forgotten or bypassed may even be why a country church has survived.

Just as America's melting pot may be more of a mosaic, there is no specific single example that would satisfy everyone's idealized version of the country church. Everybody has,

ALNA MEETINGHOUSE, LINCOLN COUNTY, MAINE
Built in 1789 when Maine was still a part of Massachusetts, the meetinghouse served as the town church for almost a century. It is still used for town meetings and the occasional wedding.

MASON'S BEND COMMUNITY CENTER & CHURCH, MASON'S BEND, ALABAMA
Designed and built by architecture students, Mason's Bend effectively employs recycled materials (the glass is composed of Chevrolet Caprice windshields).

however, a definite image of the rural house of worship in his or her mind's eye. For many, it is a white frame rectangular box with a steeple, or perhaps a stone chapel with stained glass and pointed arches. Almost all would include an adjoining, shaded cemetery containing several generations of forebears whose marble and granite markers bear reassuring symbols, whether crosses, Stars of David, Masonic emblems, or weeping willows.

No collection of a few dozen churches can presume to tell the story of the American country church. Nevertheless, the examples gathered in American Country Churches do represent a range of styles, places, and ethnic backgrounds. But this is also an attempt to reveal the craftsmanship and the care lavished on the smaller, sometimes jewel-like country chapels. By bringing together these churches, some of which are incredibly beautiful and many of which have quintessential rural settings, this book can suggest part of the story and demonstrate the richness of our country church heritage.

These churches do include a variety of affiliations, but it would be equally difficult to relate the story of America's many denominations through these few examples. One could, however, teach a credible history of the United States employing these churches as guideposts, themes, or illustrations.

The missions of the Southwest speak of Spain's attempts to claim the New World and to "Christianize" the Indians, but the missionary urge was not limited to the Church of Rome. Protestants had their share of proselytizing zeal, as seen in the Presbyterian mission for the Choctaw at Wheelock, the Episcopal church in Minnesota for the Dakota, or the Methodists in what became West Virginia.

By following the movement of those who came here in search of religious freedom, these churches could plot our demographic history. The Wends fled to Texas from Brandenburg, while the Quakers of North Carolina moved to Ohio to avoid slavery, and the Cumberland Island slaves

escaped from the plantations. Moravians and the Scotch-Irish fanned out from Pennsylvania, and the Welsh came in. Czechs, Norwegians, and just about every other European nationality headed to the Great Plains and prairies in search of farmland; Slovak miners went to Washington. Vacation chapels reveal the summer migrations of the well-to-do.

Having noted that immigrants resisted cultural assimilation, the churches themselves point to far less variety in building types than there were nationalities. There is, in fact, what one might even call an architectural melting pot—the similarities are greater than the differences. There is no easy answer for this. Although climate, practicality, and economics are all contributors, style and fashion may be the major determinant. This is reflected in the fact that during its lifetime a church may be used by different denominations with remarkable theological flexibility.

An attempt to group these churches into categories is almost self-defeating. Nevertheless, certain threads do run through the patchwork quilt that is the American country church.

For example, settlers attempted to replicate the buildings they knew back home. Englishmen from wood-building regions tended to construct wooden churches, even though their New England fields were full of stone, just as brick-building countrymen favored masonry in Maryland and Virginia. Thus, it is no surprise that Spaniards would bring with them the Baroque style of the Iberian Peninsula. Yet, cultural habits often had to be modified in the face of environment. Englishmen gave up thatching their roofs after a Massachusetts winter or two, while Franciscan builders in the desert substituted adobe for stone. Practicality, too, had a way of challenging long-held constructional traditions. Although brought here by the Swedes and Finns, everyone saw the value of the easily built and strong log cabin—it and the German hillside barn were adapted to the point of ubiquity.

MASON'S BEND COMMUNITY CENTER AND CHURCH, MASON'S BEND, ALABAMA
Permanently open and performing the function of the village church for centuries, the church is a visible symbol of hope for this poor agricultural community.

Crude structures formed the first churches. Rehoboth Church in West Virginia or the Norwegian Hauge Log Church in Wisconsin exemplify the first church buildings of so many settlers. But as soon as possible, newcomers turned to erecting a more permanent church, and as likely as not it looked as much as they could make it like the last church in which they had worshiped in England or Germany or Bohemia. Some early ecclesiastical structures, such as Saint James Episcopal Church in South Carolina, the Old Ship Meeting House in Hingham, Massachusetts, and the Bethabara Moravian Church in North Carolina, were close to their old-world models.

The most basic thread of the American church might well be the meetinghouse. The plain rectangular houselike box, as built by the Conanicut Friends Meeting in Rhode Island, is not so different from the several meetinghouses built by Moses Johnson for the Shakers. The Quaker meetinghouse in Mount Pleasant, Ohio, is not unlike that in Rockingham, Vermont. The Vermont example is one of a string of New England meetinghouses of the late eighteenth century—the so-called second meetinghouse type (to differentiate from the square, blocky first type, of which few remain), such as those in Alna, Maine, Amesbury, Massachusetts, and Sandown in New Hampshire.

Take the second meetinghouse type and relocate the altar or pulpit to one end, change its orientation by moving the main entrance from the side to the opposite end, and then add a steeple over the entrance. Acworth, New Hampshire, is a classic example of this—Rockingham with a tower, as it were. The steepled meetinghouse is one of the most abiding of American forms of worship. It becomes the basic American church: Phippsburg Congregational Church in Maine, Welsh Hill Church in Pennsylvania, Wheelock Mission Presbyterian

Church in Oklahoma, or the Lutheran churches of the High Plains. The Czech Catholic church in Praha, Texas, the Russian Orthodox temple in Wilkeson, Washington, and even the synagogue in Port Gibson, Mississippi, fit the steepled meetinghouse category.

The steeple might be the signpost, symbol, or beacon, but with or without it, many American churches are preaching boxes: a rectangular space for services, with or without ornament. Strip the steeple from Telemarken or Phippsburg or Cades Cove and it becomes the preaching box. But so many never got beyond this simple frame box—the Model T Ford of worship: the Black churches of the Mississippi Delta, like that at Shaw or the one built by former slaves on Cumberland Island, Georgia. And the best new churches are often those that acknowledge earlier traditions: the Rural Studio's Alabama church, Irving Gill's re-creation of a Spanish mission, or George Nakashima's monastery chapel in New Mexico. Admittedly, there are some wonderfully dramatic churches constructed with modern materials, but by and large Americans do not like to alter tradition.

All this simplicity does not mean that elaborateness is not appreciated, as the painted churches of Texas (both Lutheran and Catholic) or the rich altars in missions like Laguna in New Mexico and Carmel along California's Camino Real demonstrate. But there is also a thread that we might call the Anglican tradition. The Church of England, or the Episcopal Church as we call it in the United States, has perhaps been the denomination most interested in church design as artistic statement and where physical appearance assumes a greater importance.

One of our cherished myths is that eighteenth-century American Protestant churches were less cluttered and somehow more honest than their Anglican counterparts. The inference was that Tories worshiped with more foppery, while

American revolutionaries were egalitarian, no-nonsense people, in rebellion against Church of England forms. Yet, while Old North Church in Boston (of Paul Revere fame) is a meetinghouse with a steeple, it is also Episcopal (its proper name is Christ Church). The Church of England in the early eighteenth century, in Britain and elsewhere, was preaching oriented, as can be seen at Yeocomico in Virginia or Saint James Episcopal in South Carolina or Old Saint Paul's in Narragansett, Rhode Island.

Thus, we see once again that fashion is more important than denominational considerations. Touro Synagogue in Newport, Rhode Island, was the design source for Trinity Church in Brooklyn, Connecticut. Yet Touro was designed by a Quaker-turned-Anglican who based his Jewish temple on the churches of James Gibbs, an Italian-trained, Roman Catholic Scotsman practicing in London. Trinity was financed and constructed by an Anglican who refused to pay his share for the building of a new Congregational church (the state religion in Connecticut then). That classic New England meetinghouse became Connecticut's first Unitarian church in 1816. In 1865 Trinity built a church closer to the center of the village, and that Gothic Revival stone church looks not unlike a parish church in an English village.

The parish church manner was another example of the importance of style—in this case a revival of medieval forms by Anglicans in England reacting to the preaching-box Low Church Protestantism of the eighteenth century (as, for example, Paul Revere's Christ Church). American Episcopalians got caught up in the Gothic Revival fervor and produced some of the handsomest monuments of the style. Saint Mary's in Emmorton, Maryland, was actually built from a design supplied by an English architect working in New York. Another English immigrant, Richard Upjohn, not only put the first cross atop a steeple of an American church, but provided

SAINT WENCESLAUS CHURCH, SPILLVILLE, IOWA
Erected in 1860 by Czechoslovakian immigrants and completely restored in 1985, the Czech church still contains the 1876 Pfeffer organ that composer Antonín Dvořák played here regularly during the summer of 1893, and Spillville continues to be a predominantly Czech town.

designs for poorer parishes in search of appropriate Englishness, such as those which appear in the pre–Civil War South at Prairieville, Alabama, and at Hibernia, Florida. Saint Cornelia's, the Episcopal mission for the Dakota tribe in Minnesota, is a further variation on the theme.

Styles express societal trends, and churches, as much as any other kinds of architecture, can and often do make political statements. Once banned in Puritan Massachusetts Bay, Episcopalianism became fashionable in the latter half of the nineteenth century. An English-looking church in New England was not only accepted but warmly embraced, and stained glass and battlemented towers could be found at watering places in the mountains or along the seashore. Saint Columba's, just outside Newport, was built for vacationing Philadelphia families, while Saint James' in the Catskills was a seasonal chapel for summer people from Boston. Even Faith Chapel in Jekyll Island, Georgia, while nominally nondenominational, is very much in the Episcopal mode.

In the end, considerations of style are less important than the collective meaning of the American country church. We remain entangled in our uniquely American web of wanting to honor the commitment to religious freedom while demonstrably wearing religion on our sleeves. Religion is, ultimately, a private matter. So regardless of how we choose to worship or in what language our grandparents prayed, our response to a particular church may vary. Yet taken all together, these churches do continue to tell us something important about ourselves. These churches express community—the something that is larger than our everyday concerns and to which we all belong. In reminding us of who we are, they provide a sense of security, especially in times of crisis. Most of all, they strike a chord of continuity for a nation based on the radical belief of religious freedom.

Missionary Baptist Church,
CADES COVE, TENNESSEE

There are southerners who unshakably believe that Missionary Baptist Church has the finest setting of any church east of the Rockies. Nature supports their argument, for the church is at the heart of the Great Smoky Mountains National Park. It is near the Appalachian Trail (which here demarcates the border with North Carolina) and close to the highest point in Tennessee. In modest contrast to the mountains, this simple frame building is also emblematic of thousands of Protestant churches throughout the South. Missionary Baptist is a rather unremarkable building that achieves tremendous significance as every church.

It would be hard to find a more rural or more in the-back-of-beyond place as Cades Cove, and were it not for the federal government, it might have quietly disappeared. The National Park Service, however, set aside the entire Cades Cove settlement—cabins, smokehouses, pigpens, mills, barns, corncribs, springhouses—as representative of early-nineteenth-century pioneer life. Cades Cove is still farmed—a living museum of how settlers worked on the land and made a life here on the slopes of the highest mountains in the Appalachian chain.

Cades Cove was one of the earliest settlements in the Smokies. The first cabin was built by John Oliver, a veteran of the War of 1812. Religion, of course, was a major facet of frontier life. The Primitive Baptist

HIGH IN THE MOUNTAINS and still almost as isolated when built, the Cades Cove church is a representative of the white-box Protestant church across rural America.

WITH NO ELECTRICITY, no carpeting, no paved parking lot, no decoration of any kind except for a stone cross in the church floor, Cades Cove is as pure an example of a country church as one could imagine.

Church was founded first, while Missionary Baptist was founded in 1839 when the Primitive Baptists expelled some members for favoring missionary work. These were joined by a couple of Methodist churches. Three of these churches still line the eleven-mile road that connected the farms in the Cove; all still hold services.

The white frame churches replaced earlier log structures that were outgrown late in the nineteenth century, and follow a standard rectangular configuration. The foundations are rudimentary, the gable roofs are galvanized metal, and belfries constitute the most prominent exterior feature. These were congregations without wealth or cash, so the churches are large rooms that served as community gathering places. Missionary Baptist does have the unusual feature of

an entrance porch, as well as a five-sided little choir room right behind the pulpit. It forms a sort of apse on the exterior, but inside its windows flood the pulpit with backlight in sharp contrast to the main body of the church, which has only three windows on each side.

Nothing could be plainer than the locally sawn plank walls, ceiling, and floors. Yet, Missionary Baptist Church is in the same spirit as the farm buildings of the cove: the Cable Mill drive-through barn or Tipton Oliver's cantilevered barn, for example. Spawned by necessity, whether keeping varmints from the grain or trying to lighten the farmer's load, these are utilitarian forms that have become art. The homes and cabins, the barns and outbuildings of Cades Cove, all are like the uncomplicated faith of the region's early settlers. No wonder Missionary Baptist Church is a spiritual home for many Southerners.

RECENT GRAVESTONES, like the entwined hearts, tell of 200 years of continuous settlement in "the Cove."

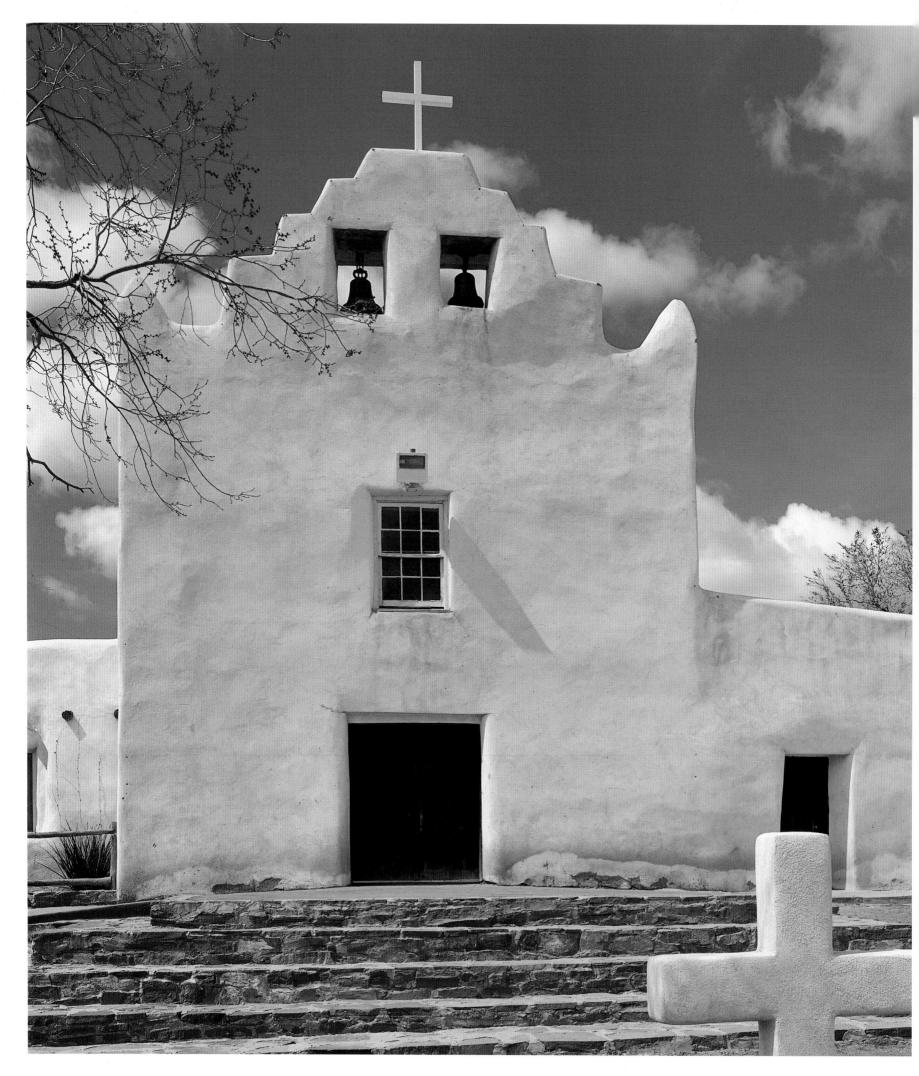

Mission San José de Laguna,
LAGUNA, NEW MEXICO

The painted image of San José behind the altar in the Laguna mission reminds us of the cultlike status of the Blessed Virgin's consort among the natives of New Mexico. Saint Joseph was venerated as a model for married men, while supplicants also prayed to him for the blessing of an easy death. Saint Barbara, who flanks the mission's patron, offered protection from sudden death, especially lightning and guns. This Roman Catholic symbolism is augmented along the nave walls by rough but energetic imagery from Pueblo mythology. These deal with the elements—thunder, rain, and the sun and the moon, as well as birds that represent the souls of people buried in the church. The wonder of Laguna is that the heavy Spanish Baroque of twisted columns and old-world iconography melds with primal animist beliefs of Indians to create a holy place with meaning for everyone.

The combination of the incredible richness of the painted and carved sanctuary and the simplicity of the walls of the rest of the mission is nothing short of astounding. In its aesthetic lineage, the sanctuary decoration reaches back through Mexico and across the ocean to Counter-Reformation Spain. Yet, the native pine was carved by an Indian with few tools and rather abstract notions of, say, canon law or the papacy. The long narrow nave and the semipolygonal sanctuary of the building itself are rooted in a Roman tradition as ancient as Saint Peter, while the Pueblos' basic adobe construction is as old as Moses in Egypt.

The New Mexico missions are simpler than those in California, and they lack the sophisticated vaulting and domes of those in Texas and Arizona. In spite of that, or maybe because of it, New Mexico's early churches are an almost perfect blend of Hispanic and Native American influences. The power of these incredibly

ALMOST CONTEMPORARY IN ITS STARK, flat adobe walls, the Laguna mission is like an abstract modern painting, and it is easy to see why so many painters and photographers were drawn to the New Mexico churches.

simple yet rich missions appeals to our modern sensibilities. Even so, the legacy of Laguna is one of conflict and subjugation, as well as of profound faith.

The dream of gold that lured explorers like Coronado to New Mexico in the sixteenth century did not come true. So the development of this dry and mountainous territory was left to a handful of incredibly brave Franciscan and Dominican friars. It was these brothers who brought new crops, cattle, and agriculture to the Indians; they also introduced Spanish colonial architecture. By the time the Puritans landed in New England, the Franciscans had built more than forty churches and converted thousands of Indians to Christianity. The alliance was not always easy, and some clerics were repressive. During the 1680 Pueblo Revolt, four hundred Spaniards and a score of priests were killed and the Spanish were driven out of New Mexico.

The Spaniards eventually returned and the pueblo at Laguna was established in 1699. Friar Antonio de Miranda directed construction of the church that was completed in 1706. Like many pueblos, Laguna was built high on a defensible bluff, even though that meant hauling the roof beams for the 105-foot-long church from as far as thirty miles away. Whether the Indian builders understood or really believed in Roman Catholicism is beyond the point. Spaniards and Indians held different ideas of the nature of the universe. But at a place like Laguna those different visions of the universe came together as a supreme artistic achievement in American art.

PAINTINGS OF PUEBLO MYTHS share the walls with Catholic Stations of the Cross. One of the sanctuary walls is not perpendicular to the 105-foot nave, which may have been an attempt to emulate Baroque perspective.

NEW MEXICO MISSIONS lacked vaults, arches, and domes, so the horizontal structural beams had elaborately carved supporting blocks. Itinerant craftsmen known as *Santeros* carved the statuary and holy figures of native pine.

Se acabo el Año de 1811. dia 6 de Agosto

MISSIONS WERE MORE than just churches, and their defensive walls sheltered other institutions (in the same way as the medieval monastery), including offices, schools, dormitories, and gardens.

Saint Columba's Chapel,

MIDDLETOWN, RHODE ISLAND

Saint Columba's honors the sixth-century Irish missionary who planted Christianity in Scotland. Its other
name, the Berkeley Memorial Chapel, remembers
another great proselytizer, George Berkeley, Bishop of
Derry, who spent three years here on Aquidneck
Island while trying to interest the British crown in
supporting a college for Blacks and Indians in the
New World. (Although he was unsuccessful in this
venture, a university in California does perpetuate his
name.) A stone from the bishop's cathedral of Saint
Colman at Cloyne is embedded in the entrance porch
at Saint Columba's, one of many links to the British
Isles in this small country church next to the sea.

The Episcopal Church in the late nineteenth century was overtaken with a wave of Anglophilia—Saint
Columba's, with its lych gate, bell cote, and picturesque
cemetery could hardly be more English. Nevertheless,
this evocation of England's green and pleasant land is
more than a mere exercise in nostalgia (many of the
enormous mansions built by robber barons in nearby
Newport might fall into that category). Rather, Saint
Columba's continues the tradition of the thirteenth-
century rural English church as the ideal model as
espoused by the Ecclesiological Society, as seen at
Saint Mary's, Emmorton, Maryland, and especially at
Saint James the Less in Philadelphia. Wilson Eyre, the
architect of Saint Columba, was a Philadelphian who
summered in Newport from 1876 to 1889.

Eyre was one of the best American practitioners of
the Arts and Crafts movement. Born in Florence, Eyre
studied architecture at MIT and then set up practice
in Philadelphia. Although somewhat forgotten, Eyre
was a pivotal figure in the circle of artists that included
the painter Maxfield Parrish and the archaeologist-
potter Henry Mercer. Eyre and Frank Miles Day, a

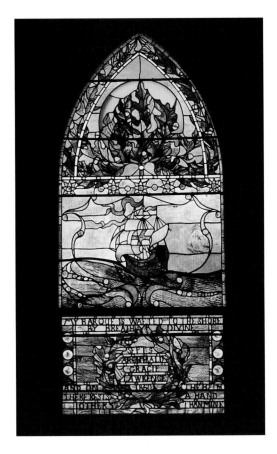

leading Collegiate Gothicist, founded *House and Garden*, perhaps the most influential design journal of the day.

As an exponent of the Arts and Crafts, Wilson Eyre was concerned with every aspect of the design—from organ case to kneelers, but it is the stained glass at Saint Columba's that truly dazzles. The windows were installed in 1885 and are examples of the opalescent, proto–Art Nouveau fashion associated with Louis Comfort Tiffany. Tiffany manufactured most of the windows here, but all but one were designed by D. Maitland Armstrong (the shimmering blue west window, *Mary Devlin Booth holding a dove*, was one of S. P. Belcher's Mercury Mosaics). Armstrong's jewel-like nave windows are utterly charming, not least of all the one with a wave-tossed sailboat on the waves: "My barque is wafted to the shore by breaths Divine, and on the helm rests a hand other than mine."

Saint Columba's communicants were nothing if not artistic and wealthy (the land, church design, furnishings, and windows were all donated). The actor Edwin Booth summered nearby and is memorialized with a plaque in the church. Saint Columba's cemetery is a pantheon of turn-of-the-twentieth-century artists, architects, and the artistically inclined. Among others, here lies the Victorian Gothic architect Edward Tuckerman Potter and classicist John Russell Pope, designer of the Jefferson Memorial and the National Gallery in Washington, D.C. A Chinese admiral sleeps not far from mural painter Allyn Cox. Joseph Lindon Smith, painter, Egyptologist, and advisor to grand dame Isabella Stewart Gardner, and his wife Corinna are buried near their friends Raphael and Elise Pumpelly. The recumbent statue of the Harvard geologist has been stolen, but Mrs. Pumpelly's bronze figure does as much as any one memorial to create the elegiac flavor of an English churchyard.

THE INSIDE OF SAINT COLUMBA'S seems more Isle of Wight than Rhode Island. The stained glass casts a warm glow over the rubble walls and wooden ceiling. The single west window is a memorial to the wife of actor Edwin Booth and the sister-in-law of John Wilkes Booth.

First African Baptist Church,

CUMBERLAND ISLAND, GEORGIA

Cumberland Island is not unlike Jekyll Island to the north. It was a popular vacation spot for the wealthy (Andrew Carnegie's brother bought 4,000 acres here in 1881), and there was a private hunting and fishing club. Nevertheless, this largest, most isolated, and least developed of the Sea Islands has a much longer history, and one that has a sadder and less prosperous side. The First African Baptist Church in the village of Half Moon Bluff is one of the simplest houses of worship imaginable and, in terms of resources, one of the poorest.

Cumberland Island's blacks were brought in as slaves to harvest the area's famed Sea Island cotton. Before there were plantations, there was the requisite fort to protect English settlers from the Spanish, while oyster-shell middens and a burial mound speak of several thousand years of aboriginal habitation before that.

WHAT THE CUMBERLAND ISLAND congregation lacked in resources it made up in faith, and this wee house of worship shows that the trappings of religion can be just that.

A grateful state of Georgia awarded a plantation to General Nathanael Greene, and it was his widow who built Dungeness in 1803 (another Revolutionary War hero, Lighthorse Harry Lee, the father of Robert E. Lee, died at Dungeness while fleeing creditors). The growing of cotton was not conducive to leisure seekers, but after the Civil War plantations were taken over by outsiders, like Carnegie's brother, five of whose children built vacation homes here. In the 1890s a hotel was opened, connected to the wharf by a mule-drawn railway. The hotel became a clubhouse in 1902, but the inaccessible island remained home to only a few families and was never developed. Today, it is part of the Cumberland Island National Seashore.

When the hotel came, small house lots were sold to blacks living in a settlement called Half Moon Bluff (the idea was to assure a loyal and permanent group of hotel workers). These former slaves and their descendents had stayed on Cumberland as squatters; they went on to develop a thriving, if less than wealthy, community of a dozen wooden structures, three cemeteries, and the First African Baptist Church.

The current church replaces a nineteenth-century log version that also served as the village school, but the modest structure is less important than what it symbolizes: First African Baptist Church represents the triumph of a dispossessed people who clung to the land, crafted their own homes, and fashioned a life around their religious faith. The church is a plain frame box perched upon concrete blocks. It has three windows on each side and one behind the altar, as well as a pressed-tin roof. Painted white inside and out, the church has no decorative touches whatsoever. Built from recycled wood in 1937, the church has no steeple, no organ, no stained-glass windows. The church's very remoteness, not to mention its austerity, appealed to John F. Kennedy Jr. and Carolyn Bessette, who wanted to marry in a place completely removed

THE CORNERSTONE IS THE ONLY exterior decoration, but it serves as an important reminder of community continuity. The stark simplicity of the chancel is breathtaking in its directness.

from the public eye. Despite the instant fame that resulted from that 1996 celebrity wedding, First African Baptist Church should not be perceived as a clichéd example of the picturesque side of Southern poverty. Rather, Miss Bessette's Narciso Rodriguez gown should be seen as a perfect complement to the church's simplicity and dignity.

THE **NOBILITY OF THE** First African Baptist church makes steeples, stained glass, and organs seem superfluous.

Acworth Meeting House,

ACWORTH, NEW HAMPSHIRE

A cworth Meeting House is the highest church in the state of New Hampshire. From its prospect at the end of the town green, the land falls away toward the scattered houses of the village below. The church looks out over a seemingly unspoiled wilderness. There is more forest and less open grazing land today, but the population of Acworth cannot have changed much since the church was erected in 1821. The southern horizon is marked by the distinctive sleeping-lion shape of Mount Monadnock, the country's tallest freestanding mountain and an object of worship by Indians and of adoration by the Transcendentalists and landscape painters.

Acworth's original settlers were pioneers from Connecticut who came here in the 1760s; Scotch-Irish from Londonderry, New Hampshire, and Yorkshiremen via Massachusetts followed soon after. By 1772, the town had voted to set aside land for a common, a meetinghouse, and a cemetery, but a minister was not called until after the Revolutionary War. The town's third preacher, Phineas Cooke, raised the current meetinghouse. Both church and town were still one in 1813 when Reverend Cooke came to Acworth, and he survived the separation six years later, but his pro-temperance views cost him his job in 1829.

The irony of Phineas Cooke's dismissal is that the magnificent church whose construction he oversaw

ACWORTH EPITOMIZES the classic New England church. A white meetinghouse with a towering steeple at the head of a town green is a typical image of Puritan theocracy and Yankee design.

USING ONLY THE SIMPLEST of tools and employing inventive decorative elements, the carpenters of Acworth created a facade of exceptional sophistication, as the central Palladian window shows.

was built by local men paid in New England rum. It must have been powerful stuff, indeed, as Acworth's meetinghouse is a remarkable architectural achievement. There are plenty of handsome nineteenth-century New England houses of worship with prominent steeples, but Acworth's front facade and tower are exceptional in inspiration and execution, and of erudition unusual for a small upcountry village.

The year 1821 marks the height of the Federal style, that delicate and decoratively inventive last phase of Georgian, and which found its finest expression in New England. The graceful pilasters of the projecting central pavilion frame an entrance group of three doors, one topped by an elliptical fanlight. The second story features an elaborate Palladian window, and an oval lunette in the pediment. All this is but prelude to the four-stage steeple, complete with balustrades, urns, pilasters, and a weathervane, that equals the best of Sir Christopher Wren's London churches. There is a strong debt to Wren, via the builders' guides of Connecticut Valley native Asher Benjamin and which the builder, Elias Carter, undoubtedly consulted. Acworth is actually the fifth of a run of six similar churches designed by Carter, beginning in Templeton, Massachusetts, in 1811.

Acworth Meetinghouse is especially unusual in that it boasts a well-preserved 1886 Victorian interior, complete with period stained glass, grained pews, and

dark trim. Thirty years earlier the ceiling had been lowered, perhaps as a way to save heat. But it was definitely a desire to be up-to-date when artist W. H. Henry stenciled flowers on the walls as part of a blue, gold, tan, red, and brown color scheme. This unexpected space comes as a bit of a shock, but it does show changes in taste and the kind of makeover many country churches would have liked to undertake.

There is a vestibule outside the doors to the sanctuary, by the rope pull for the Paul Revere bell, and lit by the Palladian window. More than any other part of the church, this shaped, whiter-than-white space captures the sense of early New England religious faith. It looks like one of those meticulous seventeenth-century paintings of a Dutch church, and the clarity of light strongly evokes the spirit of the Reformation that brought settlers to a frontier like Acworth.

THE CLARITY OF PURE LIGHT was abandoned for Victorian color, yet the surprising transformation made Acworth a most unusual church. Two giant stoves were added around 1830.

Hauge Log Church,

DANE COUNTY, WISCONSIN

The Hauge Log Church in the Blue Mounds of Wisconsin honors a Norwegian who never saw America, but whose preaching had a singular influence on Lutheranism in America. Hans Nielsen Hauge was plowing his father's fields on April 5, 1796, when he had a mystical experience not unlike the ecstasies of Roman Catholic saints. Believing that every man has the right to preach the gospel, Hauge's evangelism began to attract a large following. His pietism was not warmly received by the upper classes and the state church, and Hauge was jailed numerous times. As a peasant, Hauge's religious teachings paralleled social and political upheaval throughout Europe: Enlightenment ideas of democracy were challenging the old order.

The first great wave of Scandinavian migration in the nineteenth century carried Hauge's populist religious views to the American Midwest. The log church was not only a very early Wisconsin church (the state had only been in the Union for four years), but it was actually built together by followers of the official Norwegian state church and the Haugeans. Each person donated logs and labor, and the church held its first service in May of 1852. Alas, both sects bickered over the church, alternately locking each other out, until the non-Evangelicals built their own meeting-house in nearby Daleyville.

Although quite small (twenty by twenty feet), the church served the Hauge congregation for thirty-five years. Then the clapboard-sheathed log structure remained abandoned and unused until 1927 when a plan to move the church to Luther College in Decorah, Iowa, inadvertently stirred local Lutheran pride. The log church stayed and became the object of one of the earliest restoration projects in the state.

THE PLAINNESS OF THIS clapboard-covered log church only hints at this house of worship's important role in Norwegian-American life.

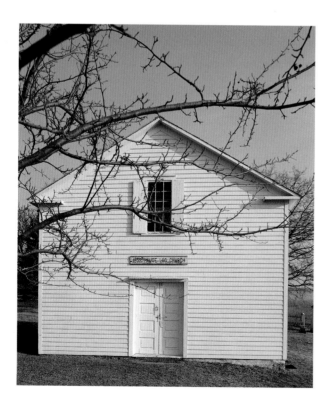

Stabilization might be a better word than restoration: the oak logs needed some new clapboards and the interior lime plaster was renewed, but the original rough pews, pulpit, and altar railing are still in place. The rural setting, too, hasn't changed much, although the Hauge Church Preservation Association is trying to save the long-distance views of the church from development.

There was another Norwegian settlement at Mount Horeb, not far from the Hauge church and founded five years later. Now known as Little Norway, this tourist destination has log houses and a re-creation of a stave church, the glorious Norwegian equivalent of the great Gothic cathedrals. This particular "stavekirke" was built in Trondheim and shipped to Chicago where it served as the Norwegian pavilion at the World's Columbian Exposition of 1893 before ending up in Wisconsin. There is no denying the charm and symbolism of this example of intricate Norse joinery and carving. The spirit-chasing dragon heads may be echoes of the fearful prows of Viking ships, but they are not nearly as powerful as the simple farmers' church interior. The Hauge pulpit is tall so that the preacher can look even those seated in the balcony right in the eye. There is nothing to distract from the evangelical spirit of Hans Nielsen Hauge.

WISCONSIN'S ROLLING HILLS and arable farmland must have seemed like heaven to immigrants from Norway's narrow valleys and rocky soil.

THE RURAL CHURCHES OF NORWAY are remembered here, and there is no extraneous decoration to distract worshipers from the Word of the Lord.

THE FOUNT OF EVANGELICAL Norwegian Lutheranism, the Hauge Log Church looks today as it did when built a century and a half ago.

Saint Mary's Church of the Assumption,
PRAHA, TEXAS

*T*he Revolutions of 1848 sent a lot of emigrants from Europe to America, especially from the Austro-Hungarian Empire. One usually thinks of the wave of Germans that settled cities like Cincinnati and St. Louis, but Germans, Czechs, Slovaks, and other central Europeans fanned out to rural areas in search of an agrarian promised land. A penniless Matthias Novak arrived in Mulberry, Texas, in 1854. He saved enough money to buy 100 acres, changed the name of the town to Praha (Czech for Prague), and created the mother colony of Czech settlements in the Texas hill country. Father Joseph Bithowski built a frame church in Praha in 1865; two other churches followed. By 1890 the community embarked on building the large limestone church that dominates the village today.

Saint Mary's—the first of three Czech Catholic churches built in Fayette County—must have represented a considerable sacrifice on the part of its Bohemian farmers. Praha started to decline following the laying of the Southern Pacific Railroad a few miles away. Even as the town emptied (it has about two dozen inhabitants now), the symbolic position of the church grew, and thousands of people return to a Czech homecoming every Feast of the Assumption. Saint Mary's is also preeminent among the dozen "painted" churches of this part of Texas.

The 130-foot steeple makes Praha something of a landmark, while the stone walls are quite uncommon hereabouts. The side walls were stuccoed in 1930, highlighting the stone buttresses, doorways, and pointed-arch windows, all giving the Gothic church a rather un-Texas-like appearance. Spiky Gothic skylines dot the prairies from Texas to the Dakotas, but what really makes Saint Mary's so unusual is its lively painted interior, where Gothic becomes Baroque.

SAINT MARY'S STEEPLE announces the Czech presence on the prairie, but its stone Gothic walls give no indication of its rich interior.

Having expended considerable expense and effort to secure masonry for their church walls, the parishioners wanted something of their old home inside the new church. As providence would have it, a Swiss painter by the name of Gottfried Flury had settled nearby in 1895, just as the church was being finished. Flury had immigrated to New York as a teenager and worked as a house painter and theatrical-scenery painter. In Texas, he would make a career as a mural and church painter (and later even secured the contract to do all the billboards in Travis County), but Praha was his first big break.

The entire church is painted. Octagonal columns are marbleized with gold specks, the beaded-board ceiling was painted blue to serve as a metaphorical sky, while trompe l'oeil banding looks like ribbed vaults. Three angels, wearing ochre, pink, and blue robes, soar over the altar; beneath them are representations of two churches back in Prague. The vaults of the side aisles feature abundant flora and fauna, no doubt suggesting Paradise.

Father Netardus applied additional ornamentation following his appointment in 1901; he is responsible for the life-size painting of the Slavic Saints Cyril and Methodius. Over the years, both statuary and painting have needed restoration, much of it done by Gene Mikulik, who tended Saint Mary's and other churches nearby. Mikulik created Our Lady of Victory, in which the Virgin hovers over the nine members of this tiny parish who were killed in one year during World War II.

A SWISS STAGE-SET PAINTER created one of the most magnificent painted interiors in Texas. Floral designs and depictions of remembered Czech churches open up a heaven-like sky.

THE LANDSCAPE IS EAST Texas, but the names in the cemetery recall Bohemia's forests and meadows.

Saint James Episcopal Church,
GOOSE CREEK, SOUTH CAROLINA

SAINT JAMES IS A DESIGN of remarkable sophistication; high style from London with a Caribbean flavor.

*L*egend holds that the royal coat of arms spared the little church at Goose Creek from being sacked by invading British troops. Whether or not the rampant lion and unicorn flanking the Hanoverian crest prominently displayed over the pulpit really acted as a deterrent, Saint James Episcopal Church could not be more English. Although located in the swampy plantation country inland from Charleston, the elaborate east end, with its wineglass pulpit, suspended sounding board, and luxuriant Corinthian pilasters, not to mention the royal arms, must have seemed very familiar to the English soldiers. South Carolina may have been the back of beyond to them, yet the richness of Saint James would not have been out of place in a contemporary London church.

Saint James Episcopal Church was built by planters who came to the Carolina Low Country from the Caribbean island of Barbados, the wealthiest of Britain's American Colonies. The provincial government had officially established the Church of England in South Carolina, and Saint James was one of the nine original parishes. Construction of the church itself was supported by the Society for the Propagation of the Gospel in Foreign Parts—the Society's emblem of a mother pelican piercing her breast to feed her young adorns the pediment over the main entrance.

THE CENTRAL POSITION of the wineglass pulpit shows the dominance of the sermon in early eighteenth century Church of England services. The nearly square interior, complete with Corinthian capitals and the Royal Arms, is as elaborate as any contemporary church in London.

Goose Creek was close to Charleston and the land was rich, and so Saint James's elaborate decoration and stucco finish bespoke a plantation plutocracy. The architectural promise of the church, however, was not echoed in the life of the parish. Early ministers had to be imported from England, and both they and the planters preferred nearby Charleston society, close to the sea and away from malarial swamps. When completed in 1719, the church had seventy whites and eight blacks as communicants, while three decades later there were only two dozen whites and as many blacks. The church simply wasn't a going parish, and the building was used only occasionally. Yet, Saint James has always been treasured as one of the most notable colonial American houses of worship; it has been maintained and periodically restored.

Saint James reflects the taste and knowledge of its patrons, even though such architectural sophistication at so early a date was remarkable. The colored stucco may have a Barbadian flavor, but the round-headed windows with their heavy surrounds, the quoins on the corners, and the full entablature of the main doorway are as up-to-date as any London church by Sir Christopher Wren or his even more Baroque contemporary, James Gibbs. The farther Englishmen roam from home, the more English are their cultural aspirations.

Saint James is small—only forty by fifty feet—yet these dimensions are significant. The main worship space east of the rear gallery is almost a perfect square. Anglican worship was more Protestant, more preaching oriented in the early eighteenth century, as the centrally located pulpit makes clear. But the emphasis here is less theological than architectural: in its geometrical abstraction, Saint James Episcopal Church recalls the best of Wren's churches, like Saint Stephen, Walbrook, in London.

SAINT JAMES, GOOSE CREEK, is an intellectual exercise in graceful and elegant proportions. It has remained one of America's notable churches for almost three centuries.

San Carlos Borroméo de Carmelo Mission,
CARMEL, CALIFORNIA

How can one not avoid the awesome weight of history at the mission in Carmel? California's colonial history is completely intertwined with the string of missions that ran from Mexico to the Golden Gate. But San Carlos Borroméo de Carmelo was the home mission and the administrative capital of the Franciscan effort to Christianize California and secure it against development by the Russians and the English. The mission was appropriately named for Charles Borromeo, the Milanese bishop and daystar of the Counter-Reformation. The settlement of the entire American Southwest was part of that worldwide movement to reform the Roman Catholic Church following the Protestant Reformation.

The founder of San Carlos and the friar almost single-handedly responsible for the success of the Spanish in California was Father Junípero Serra. One expects exemplary faith in a missionary priest in an alien land, but Serra was one of the most remarkable figures in American history. The Majorcan friar had tremendous executive ability, as well as force of personality: he founded nine missions in a decade and a half, made thousands of converts to Catholicism, and introduced ranching and farming husbandry that established California's agricultural future. Father Serra was buried at San Carlos in 1784, ensuring the mission's role as a place of pilgrimage.

The mission beneath whose floor Serra lies is, in fact, a later building—the work of another great mission builder, Fermín de Lasuén. Serra's successor also founded nine missions, but at San Carlos he built in stone instead of adobe, as clearly this was to be a monument to Serra and the Franciscans. Architecturally, the California mission churches are less splendid than those in Texas, though not as plain as those in New Mexico. While a handful of the Pacific Coast churches were made of

SAN CARLOS WAS BUILT in honor of and as the final resting place for Father Junípero Serra, the guiding force behind the establishment of Spanish missions in California.

THE MEXICAN BUILDER of San Carlos created a soaring vaulted nave by placing stone ribs on massive stone walls. Although once abandoned, it has been restored as a major monument to the settlement of California.

stone, San Carlos is the most ambitious, and its use of a vaulted nave makes it unique.

The friars were usually their own architects, but Fray Lasuén hired a mason named Manuel Estevan Ruiz, who was certainly familiar with the architectural landscape of Mexico. Ruiz showed the Native Americans how to quarry and dress the soft local limestone, and they completed the mission in four years (1797). Springing from the seven-foot thick walls, transverse ribs of stone support a vaulted ceiling. Although the arched ceiling itself was constructed of wood (which makes more sense in the earthquake-prone Bay Area), the vaulting demonstrated a sophistication that transcended local limitations and called up memories of Baroque Spain.

Other old-world "genetic coding" contributed to the church's broad, asymmetrical facade. The interlaced star-shaped quatrefoil windows, the outline of the egg-shaped dome over the campanile, and the patio with its fountains and flowers, have a Moorish flavor. The Arabic culture of Granada, Cordoba, and Serra's native Majorca, banished from Spain at the time of Columbus, reappears in Carmel.

Following the independence of Mexico and the secularization of the missions, the Indians drifted away, the friars were gone, and decay was the order of the day. San Carlos was virtually a ruin. There were several restorations—1884, 1924, and again in the 1930s. While only the church and the connected convento of the mission complex were rebuilt, it was important to Californians to preserve this West Coast equivalent of Independence Hall. In 1961, Pope John XXIII declared San Carlos Borroméo a Minor Basilica. Such recognition was only further confirmation of Carmel's beloved place in the continuum of Spanish missionary history.

THE COVERED ARCADE connecting church and convento is a descendant of the Roman courtyard house, the medieval cloister, and the Hispano-Moresque patio, as well as the forerunner of the Bay Area modernist house.

Friends Meeting House,

MOUNT PLEASANT, OHIO

Like the tenets of their faith, the Society of Friends' meetinghouses tend to be unadorned. That at Mount Pleasant has no painted walls, no religious icons of any kind, and virtually no detailing other than what was absolutely necessary. When Quaker minister Jacob Ong designed this brick pile in 1814, he was simply repeating the basic denominational pattern of rectangular block with steep gable roof and a symmetrical, bilateral bay treatment that reflected the practice of separating men and women at service. This house of worship could just as easily be in eastern Pennsylvania as on the Western frontier.

The Mount Pleasant meetinghouse, however, happens to be ninety by sixty-two feet and able to seat more than two thousand people on plain benches and canted balconies. This astoundingly large hall can be divided by means of a paneled partition that is rolled up onto a capstan in the attic when not in use (it takes four men to do this). Seemingly as isolated now as it was two centuries ago, this is clearly no ordinary place. Mount Pleasant was more than just the first yearly meeting west of the Alleghenies, it was the beachhead for the Quakers and Quaker influence for all of America west of here. It is also a significant monument in the struggle against slavery.

Built only a few years after Ohio became a state, Mount Pleasant served as yearly meeting for Friends throughout western Pennsylvania, all of Ohio, and into the Indiana Territory. By 1826 it served 8,873 members and fifty-three congregations. The village that grew up around the meeting was a monument to the ingenuity and commercial savvy of the Quakers and their Scotch-Irish neighbors. It was the largest wheat market in pre-canal Ohio. And, reflecting enlightened Quaker ideals, it had a public school, a

THE MOUNT PLEASANT FRIENDS MEETING was one of the earliest Quaker houses of worship in the Northwest Territories. Abolitionist sentiment was strong in Mount Pleasant and the town was an important stop on the Underground Railway.

fire department, a library, and a market house, as well as dozens of mills, including the state's only successful silk mill.

It is simply not possible to disassociate the yearly meeting from the defining issue of the nineteenth century. Mount Pleasant was only a few miles from the Wheeling slave market (then in Virginia), and the Ohio River formed the border between slave and free states. It would be accurate to describe the entire village as a station on the Underground Railway, but blacks were encouraged to stay and work here, and they felt safe in Mount Pleasant. The Friends founded a school for freed black children by 1817 and during the 1840s and 1850s ran a Free Labor Store that sold nothing produced by slaves. Eventually, members of the black population established an African Methodist church, while five blacks fought in "colored regiments" in the Civil War.

One of the first abolitionist newspapers in the nation, *The Philanthropist*, began printing in Mount Pleasant in 1817, followed a few years later by *Genius of Universal Emancipation*. Most important, the meetinghouse was the site of the second Ohio Anti-Slavery Convention in 1837. One associates the Society of Friends with an unparalleled commitment to pacifism and antislavery, and, in fact, Mount Pleasant's founders were themselves refugees from the South, where their refusal to own slaves made them pariahs. In 1800, an entire meeting walked from North Carolina to Ohio—the kind of spirit that would lead to the building of Mount Pleasant's Friends Meeting House.

DESPITE ITS UNPREPOSSESSING exterior, Mount Pleasant could hold over two thousand people; it was the site of the Ohio Anti-Slavery Convention in 1837. An ingenious screen could be raised to double the size of the meeting hall.

Saint Margaret's Church of Hibernia,
GREEN COVE SPRINGS, FLORIDA

T he St. Johns River drains much of northern Florida. Its banks, flanked by antebellum mansions and orange groves, attracted the first wave of northerners to places like St. Augustine, Jacksonville, and Green Cove Springs. In the late nineteenth century, developers and moneyed visitors like J. C. Penney came to the area. Green Cove Springs even billed itself as the "Saratoga of the South," while architects from Philadelphia and Boston designed Saint Mary's Episcopal Church there. Built in 1878 with the encouragement of the bishop who had served at Wall Street's Trinity Church, it is not surprising that Anglicans would have favored the Carpenters Gothic style made popular by Trinity's architect, Richard Upjohn. Yet, it is a similar but smaller church nearby that has deep roots in an earlier Florida.

Saint Margaret's Church of Hibernia was constructed in the same year as Saint Mary's and in the same board-and-batten Rural Gothic construction. The very name Hibernia acknowledges the Irish birth of George Fleming, an orange grower who had settled here in 1783. Florida was still Spanish then; the king of Spain granted the land to Fleming, on which he developed his island plantation. That royal "pedigree" for his land, however, did not protect him from Indian attacks, swarming insects, and the boom-or-bust economics of citrus growing. By 1822, a year after George Fleming's death, Florida had become an American territory (and Jacksonville had changed its name from Cowford); Fleming's son Lewis continued the tradition of planter society through commercial contact with the outside world and a belief that education and culture were necessities of frontier life.

The plantation master's first wife, Augustina Cortes, was a descendant of Mexico's conqueror. His

SAINT MARGARET'S CHURCH sits among the orange groves that brought the first settlers to northern Florida. It is part English, part Deep South, and completely romantic.

second wife, Margaret Seton Fleming, taught Bible classes to neighbors, slaves, and visitors, and hung on after her husband's death and during the Civil War when Yankee soldiers commandeered the plantation. She opened the house to visitors as a way to make ends meet. One such visitor was Alonzo Potter, bishop of Pennsylvania, who encouraged Margaret to build a chapel, which she began in 1875. Three years later, the chapel's first service was, sadly, the funeral of Mrs. Fleming herself.

The poignancy of Margaret Fleming's story is echoed in the almost achingly beautiful setting of a Florida before development and deforestation. This narrow box of a church is quite simple, but its tall proportions (visually reinforced by the vertical board-

ing), side entrance, and tiny bell cote give the building a decidedly medieval feeling—as if an English maiden had been spirited away to a South Seas island. The narrow lancet windows are filled with stained glass, adding an even more ethereal atmosphere to the interior (both Margaret Fleming and Edwin Weed, the bishop who consecrated the chapel in 1894, are depicted in one of the windows). Hibernia seemed much unchanged for decades, and Saint Margaret's had neither rector nor parish status until recently. Ironically, the appeal of what was once the Fleming plantation has drawn more and more people, and soon a larger church will be erected here. Saint Margaret's will be maintained as a chapel—and as a living link to old Florida.

THE LITTLE CHURCH WAS VIRTUALLY a private chapel for Hibernia plantation, and was the inspiration of Hibernia's mistress Margaret Fleming, who was buried from here in 1878.

Sabbathday Lake Shaker Meeting House,

SABBATHDAY LAKE, MAINE

New Hampshire housewright Moses Johnson signed the original Enfield Covenant in 1782. At the age of thirty, the New Hampshire carpenter, his wife, and three children gave up property and conjugal rights to join the communal sect now called the Shakers. Soon thereafter, Brother Moses Johnson was asked to apply his skills to building a meetinghouse for the Shaker community at New Lebanon, New York.

The meetinghouse was always the first building constructed after a Shaker community was established, and Johnson's first design in New Lebanon worked so well it became the prototype for another nine meetinghouses in New York, Connecticut, Massachusetts, New Hampshire, and Maine. The Sabbathday Lake meetinghouse was the last of Johnson's run, but they were all very much the same. All Shaker meetinghouses were painted white—the only building in the community so colored, and all were approximately the same size (this Maine example is thirty-two by fifty-five feet). All were wood, gambrel roofed, and had seven-bay facades; the left door was for Brothers, the right for Sisters; there were two small brick chimneys at either end.

The United Society of Believers in Christ's Second Appearing was founded in England, an outgrowth of Quakerism and a mystical sect called the New Lights. Their leader, Mother Ann Lee, came to upstate New York in 1774 searching for religious freedom, land, and converts. Not only did the meetinghouse have to seat the entire community during services (150 at Sabbathday Lake's peak), it had to be both open and strong enough to handle rigorous communal dancing (the "Shaking Quakers" got their shortened name because of their shaking rituals). So, Moses Johnson's

THE SHAKER MEETING HOUSE SERVES the last active Shaker community. It was the ninth in a series of almost identical meetinghouses for other Shaker communities. In keeping with their faith, Shaker cemeteries have no headstones.

meeting space had no vertical bearing members to impede dancing; ten massive beams in concert with queen post trusses span the space and carry the weight of the floors above.

One of the most successful of many American communal experiments—there were a score of villages and 6,000 members just before the Civil War—the Shakers prospered through a combination of spirituality and hard work. While remembered today primarily for their simple yet elegant furniture—and their vows of celibacy—the Shakers were famously self-sufficient. Sabbathday Lake's 1,900 acres supported farming and light industry—flour, spinning and lumber mills, extensive orchards, and a thriving packaged-seed business. When Johnson arrived to supervise construction of the meetinghouse, the Brothers had already cut and seasoned the timbers, quarried the foundation stones, forged all of the hardware, and fired the chimney bricks.

Although quite small, Sabbathday Lake is still an active Shaker community—the last one, but its Covenant has never been closed and converts would be welcome. Thus, the meetinghouse takes on an added significance. Unlike restored or reconstructed Shaker meetinghouses, that at Sabbathday Lake is original. Services are still held here, the faith is alive.

The only known photograph of a Shaker meeting was taken at Sabbathday Lake in 1885; the room looks the same: white plastered walls, woodwork painted a bluish tint prescribed by Millennial Laws, brown raised benches for visitors from "the World." More than two hundred years later, the unpretentiousness, spareness, and holiness of Brother Moses Johnson's meetinghouse design maintains the Shaker dictum of living as if you were to die tomorrow, and working as though you were to live forever.

SINGING AND VIGOROUS DANCING characterized Shaker services; there are no vertical supports to interfere with these dances. The blue strips along the walls were lined with pegs that held chairs during dancing and cleaning.

THE BARNS REMIND US that Sabbathday
Lake is still a working community.

Coeur d'Alene
Mission of the Sacred Heart,
CATALDO, IDAHO

The Jesuits have the reputation of being the shock troops of the missionary orders. The Blackrobes, as the Indians called them, seemed physically and intellectually tougher than their gentler Franciscan brethren in the Southwest. Known for being totally fearless, they were better educated. Jesuit Anthony Ravalli, builder of the Coeur d'Alene Mission of the Sacred Heart, studied engineering, medicine, and pharmacology. He used all of his Italian training when he arrived in the West in 1844.

Father Ravalli was assigned to the Blackfeet Tribe in the Bitterroot Mountains, where he designed and built Montana's first mission, as well as a sawmill and a gristmill (the state named a county for him). But it was because of his reputation as a medicine man (he revived a hanged Indian woman, among other "miracles") that the Coeur d'Alene people of northern Idaho asked the Jesuits to send Father Ravalli to build them a mission.

Dramatically sited above the Coeur d'Alene River with a mountain backdrop, the mission lasted from 1846 to 1877 (when the tribe was moved to a reservation). The mission was an entire community—mills, repair shops, barns, cabins, lodges, and even a cemetery—much like a medieval monastery. In the militant spirit of the Counter-Reformation, the church itself was meant to impress, to be a tour de force.

Coeur d'Alene Mission is more than ninety-one feet long, forty-one feet wide, and its stepped Baroque pediment, complete with urns and a carved sunburst medallion, rises over fifty feet. Ravalli and two assistant Brothers were able to construct this church with only the simplest of tools and without any nails whatsoever. Indians harnessed to crude

A VISION OF ROME in the far-off frontier. One Jesuit priest, using Native- American labor and very few tools, built this impressive Baroque facade; the church is the oldest structure in Idaho.

trucks brought the stones and lumber; huge trees were adzed into twenty-four-foot timbers, as well as the facade's six Tuscan columns. The framing was mortised and tenoned together and then interlaced with saplings; grass was woven in the saplings, and the entire surface was spread with mud (in 1865 the church walls were clapboarded).

The scale of the church would be accomplishment enough, but through his talent and ingenuity Ravalli was able to re-create a convincing reflection of Rome. Ravalli and his Belgian assistant Brother Huybrechts created their church triumphant by using materials at hand. Walls were painted to simulate marble; fabric (purchased from the Hudson Bay trading post at Walla Walla) was painted and stretched across the walls. Statues were carved from pine logs, chandeliers were fashioned from tin cans, and facsimiles of Italian Baroque canvases were painted. The climax of this majestic space is a polygonal half-domed apse, complete with a painting by Father Ravalli of Christ and the Sacred Heart above what appears to be a marble altar.

Artistic achievement aside, Cataldo was an important mission. It was halfway between the headwaters of the Columbia and Missouri Rivers, and it served as the center of the Jesuit missions for the entire Northwest. Still, Ravalli's influence was considerable—and architecture was just one of his many resources. Under his guidance the nomadic buffalo-hunting tribe turned to farming (which he taught them), and when then neighboring Nez Percé tribe made war, the Coeur d'Alene did not join them. For their troubles, the Coeur d'Alene were sent to a reservation away from the mission. Yet they return to this sacred place every August for the Feast of the Assumption.

FR. RAVALLI TRANSFORMED a large log building into a wilderness version of an Italian Jesuit church, using paint, canvas, tin cans, and a lot of imagination.

THE MULTI-TALENTED PRIEST CREATED a domed apse of wood that resembled stucco, while he fashioned an altar of painted faux marble. The Indians revered Fr. Ravalli as miracle worker.

Telemarken Lutheran Church,

CLARK COUNTY, SOUTH DAKOTA

Telemarken is a classic example of "The Lutheran Church on the Prairie": a late-nineteenth-century white box with a steeple that, however plain, is a landmark in the flat landscape. The very Norwegian name reveals which immigrant group built it, but the Lutheran Church on the Prairie can be Danish or Swedish or Finnish, and of course German.

There were hundreds of these churches in the upper Midwest. As in preindustrial Europe, the prairie churches were every few miles apart—there were churches where there were not towns. Part of this was because of distances in the vast reaches of farmland (the Homestead Act awarded 160 acres to each newcomer), but also, the first immigrant communities tried to maintain their distinct culture and, most of all, language.

There are, unfortunately, far too many churches for the region to support. Cars, economic hard times, outmigrations of young people, and the Americanization of old languages spelled an end to many of the small communities. Churches were abandoned, and many have since disappeared; congregations joined with nearby churches in order to survive. In 1948 Telemarken joined up with Calvary Lutheran in Wallace, two and half miles away.

The cemetery is still used for occasional burials, and there is a Memorial Day service every year that beckons Norwegian Americans home. Telemarken was restored for its centennial in 1994,

HAVING TRADED ONE HARSH LAND for another, Norwegian farmers erected simple prairie churches that symbolized their commitment to the new land and their love of the old country.

THE CHURCH EQUALED COMMUNITY for many South Dakota
farmers, and was thus a key landmark in a seemingly empty land. The
white preaching-box form is enlivened by Gothic lancet windows.

for even without an active congregation it was deemed important to maintain this symbol of Norwegian settlement in northeastern South Dakota.

While the Germans made up the largest group of settlers in South Dakota, like Ireland, Norway sent a substantial number of its people to the United States in the 1800s. The conditions were much the same in both lands: rural poverty exacerbated by a population explosion, a desire for land, and a hope for freedom (Norway was then a part of Sweden and earlier had been part of Denmark). The majority of Scandinavians sought rural areas, rather than the cities that drew the Irish, along with eastern and southern Europeans. Fair-skinned Nordic peoples seamlessly assimilated into Midwestern America, but Norwegian was the language of the pulpit and Sunday school for much of the life of the church. The donor of the land was Ole Aas, the builder was

EVEN THOUGH THEY HELD on to their Norwegian roots, Telemarken's parishioners became thoroughly American and they were buried in the land which they had made their own.

Edward Holvig, Halvor Markrud added the bell tower, and B. L. Hagboe was the first pastor.

The exterior of the church—white frame, steeple, lancet windows—is standard Protestant-issue preaching box. References to Norway are inside. There was not much money to spend in 1894, so the entire inside is covered with narrow tongue-and-groove boards, including the curved ceiling. Everything is plain except for the altarpiece and pulpit. The altar is Gothic, complete with pinnacles and quatrefoils; the central feature is a painted picture of a risen Christ. The altar ensemble is the most direct link to old Norway—a fragment of the settlers' roots replanted in the American grasslands.

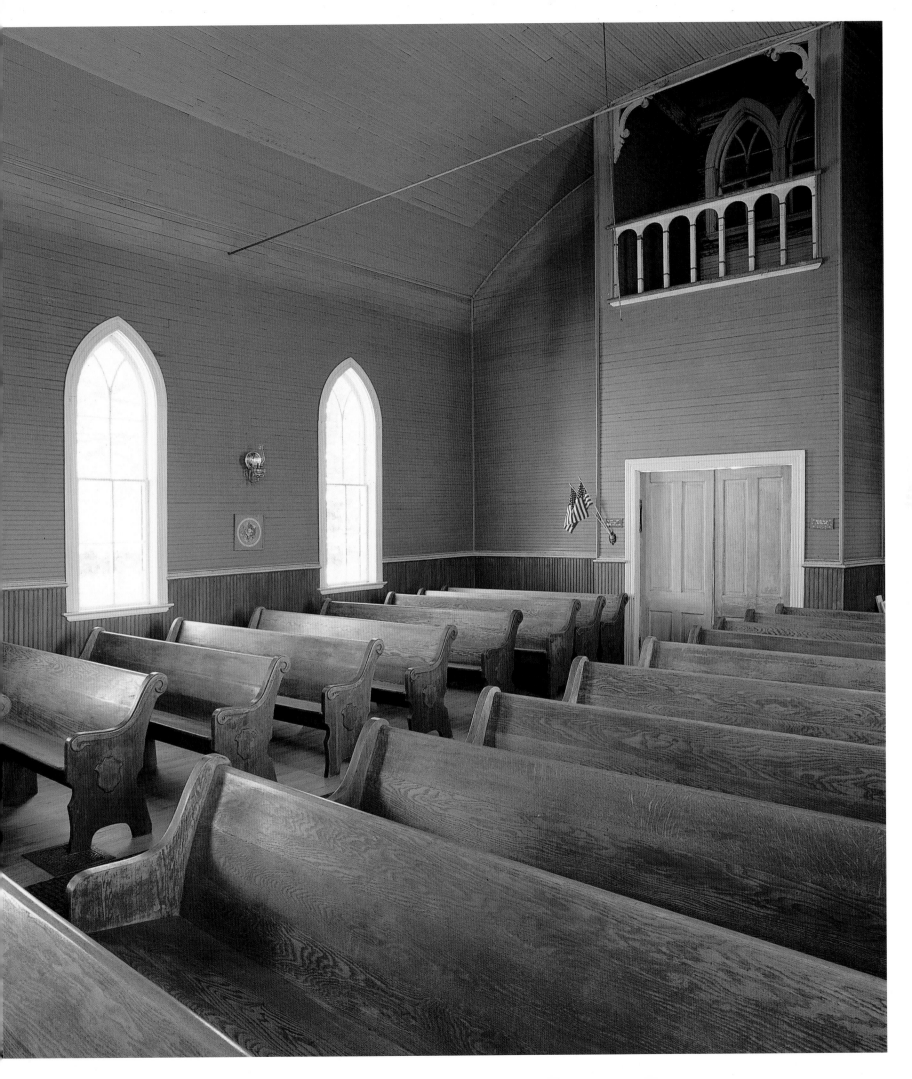

Saint Mary's Church,
EMMORTON, MARYLAND

*I*f you serendipitously chanced upon Saint Mary's in northeastern Maryland, you could be forgiven for thinking this was a perfect example of a thirteenth-century parish church brought stone by stone from the English countryside. In a way you would not be far wrong, for Saint Mary's was meant to evoke the Middle Ages, and its design was part of a conscious effort to bring the Episcopal church in line with a liturgical revival in the Church of England.

As opposed to eighteenth-century preaching-oriented churches, such as Saint James in South Carolina or Yeocomico in Virginia, Saint Mary's is one of the best examples of the Anglican Communion's desire to return to its pre-Reformation roots and to revive the liturgy, music, and art of a more "Catholic" age. The Gothic Revival caught hold in America in the 1840s, and more and more churches featured spiky picturesque skylines, surpliced choirs, and deep chancels for the celebration of the Eucharist. Architects knowledgeable in medieval forms were unable to keep up with the demand for English Gothic designs, so model plans were published and made available, particularly to smaller parishes in rural areas.

Saint Mary's is more than just a notable early example of Rural Gothic, it is actually the model church designed by architect Frank Wills and published in the *New York Ecclesiologist* in 1849. The magazine sought to

ALTHOUGH PLANTED IN the Maryland countryside, Saint Mary's was based on a "model" Rural Gothic church, one that was to give an American echo to English nineteenth-century liturgical and architectural reform.

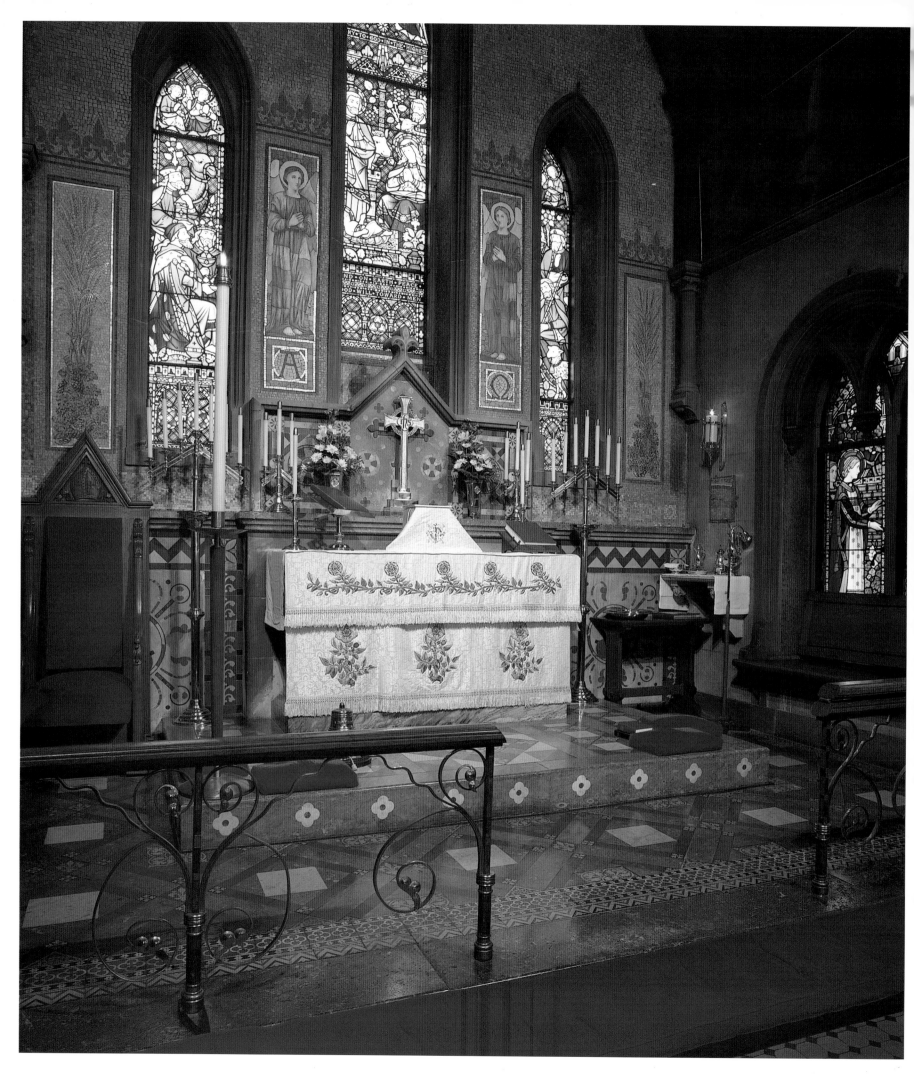

NO OTHER AMERICAN CHURCH has a complete set of stained glass windows designed by the great Victorian architect, William Butterfield. English artisans also enriched the chancel with tiles, brasses, and mosaics.

be the arbiter of Episcopal church design in this country, and the English immigrant was their architect of choice. Wills was also a friend of William Whittingham, who as Bishop of Maryland encouraged the Reverend William Francis Brand to found the church and build it according to Wills's design.

The Emmorton church remains one of the finest small Gothic Revival churches anywhere, and much of the credit must go to Brand. A New Orleans native who earned a law degree at the University of Virginia, Brand was rector at Saint Mary's from its establish-

ment in 1849 until his death fifty-six years later. Brand used family money to erect the church and was forever raising funds to embellish it; he had strong ideas on what he saw as the correct taste, and he brooked no interference from his vestry in such matters as buying stained glass and decorative fittings for his beloved church. The interior of the little granite church is marked by incredible richness, but the single-minded focus of Brand resulted in a setting of remarkable harmony.

In keeping with the English thirteenth-century

style, the window openings are simple pointed lancets, yet they are filled with glorious glass designed by arguably the most inventive British Gothic Revivalist, William Butterfield. These fifteen London-made windows chronicle the life of Christ according to Saint Luke and are the only such complete set in America. The chalice and paten were also crafted in London, while the tiles are Minton, a favorite pottery of Arts and Crafts church designers like Butterfield. Slate, different colored stone, mosaics, woodwork, brass abound, much of it bearing the Blessed Virgin's emblem, the lily.

Brand's assistant, Johannes Adam Oertel, was a Bavarian artist who fled to America in 1848 and later became a priest. Best known for his ceiling painting in the U.S. House of Representatives, Oertel carved the lectern and pulpit at Saint Mary's and created a series of chancel paintings in honor of the rector. The face of Moses in one of the paintings is none other than Brand himself.

IN CONTRAST TO the incredibly rich chancel, the nave of Saint Mary's is deliberately plain.

Mission Espíritu Santo Church,

GOLIAD, TEXAS

Nuestra Señora del Espíritu Santo de Zuñiga is one of the least known of all the Spanish mission churches in Texas. Situated along the San Antonio River about fifty miles inland of Corpus Christi, the mission is the heart of one of the Lone Star State's most historic places.

Like the Alamo, the mission in Goliad was the scene of a major and tragic battle in the Texas War of Independence. On March 18, 1836, Texans under Major James Fannin fought a skirmish with the Mexican army at the mission, and the following day they were defeated at the Battle of Coleto nearby. Fannin and 342 of his men were brought back to the mission and executed by orders of Mexican General Santa Anna. "Remember Goliad!" became a rallying cry following the Palm Sunday massacre.

The history of Goliad is not all dark (although both Confederate and Union troops occupied the mission ruins during the Civil War). The mission was established here in 1749 by Franciscans to Christianize the Aramana Tribe (the order's coat of arms—five wounds of Christ surrounded by a knotted cord—flanks the arched main doorway). The friars were successful ranchers and soon had as many as 30,000 cattle. After independence, both Baptists and Presbyterians operated schools here. But it is the Spanish colonial legacy that predominates.

Espíritu Santo has a classic mission facade: the entire composition is almost a mirror image of the San Carlos Borromeo in Carmel, California, while the details are clearly inspired by those found at San

GOLIAD, ALTHOUGH MUCH LESS known than the Alamo, was also the site of an important and equally tragic battle in the Texas War of Independence. The mission itself is actually a New Deal-era reconstruction.

GOLIAD'S BUILDERS THOROUGHLY researched mission architecture throughout Mexico and the Southwest. Historical details include the Franciscan Order's emblem—a knotted cord wrapped around Christ's wounds.

Antonio's La Purísimo Concepción. The interior of the small mission (100 by 20 feet) is almost a textbook example of the best of the Spanish Baroque interpreted by Mexican priests and Indian laborers. The ribbed vault of the thirty-foot-high nave, the tile floor, the wainscoting painted with geometric Indian designs, and the various carvings—reredos, stations of the cross, pulpit—all speak of a familiarity with the best of Texas's colonial heritage.

Not perfection perhaps, but Goliad Mission is undeniably handsome, a thoughtful and informed rendition of what a Spanish mission should be. In fact, Espíritu Santo is a reconstruction, built by the Civilian Conservation Corps (CCC) in the 1930s. Goliad County Judge and newspaper publisher James Arthur White lobbied for decades to create the proper memorial to Goliad's history. The Texas Centennial celebrations of 1936 may have been the impetus, but Roosevelt's New Deal provided the manpower, the money, and the expertise.

From 1936 to 1941, a CCC camp, along with archaeologists, historians, and architects, worked on Goliad Mission. The workmen and artists of the CCC carved the pulpit and the beams, floor tiles were fired with clay from the river, and blacksmiths re-created hinges and hardware based on archaeological finds. (During a visit to the mission in 1940, Eleanor Roosevelt commended "everyone of the fine workmanship that is in evidence everywhere.")

We might cast a scornful glance back on such "restoration," but architects who had traveled Mexico and the Southwest to search out and document the best Spanish colonial design supervised the work here. The delightful "Moorish merlins" that formed the scalloped walls of the sacristy may be just a bit fanciful, but by and large the designers formed a remarkable team intent on saving Goliad and reviving the mission's patrimony. Goliad is, indeed, something of a period piece: a tribute to Texas history, the New Deal, and the pioneering age of restoration.

Rehoboth Church,

UNION, WEST VIRGINIA

At twenty-two by twenty-nine feet, Rehoboth might well be the smallest country church imaginable, yet its role in the establishment of American Methodism was enormous. This log building not only is the oldest extant Protestant church west of the Alleghenies but also served as the heart of the missionary work on the frontier, and it was associated with the most important figure in the early Methodist Church, Francis Asbury.

Asbury preached at the dedication of the Rehoboth church in 1786, which was barely two years after the Methodists declared themselves an American denomination. John Wesley, leader of the

THIS UNASSUMING LOG CABIN is one of the key monuments in American Methodism, as it was from here that the new denomination spread into the mountains and westward. Lacking anything that might be called decoration, the interior of this pioneer church is powerful in its stark simplicity.

evangelical offshoot of the Church of England, sent Asbury to America to organize the new church. Asbury devoted the rest of his life to nurturing the roots of Wesleyanism, both as a spiritual leader and by the practical business of training preachers and ordaining them.

In 1788, Asbury conducted the first trans-Appalachian ordination at Rehoboth, from whence the new deacon based his circuit-riding ministry. The indefatigable Methodist bishop also conducted three preachers' conferences at Rehoboth in the 1790s and preached there twice in the same decade. Asbury wrote in his journal: "Thursday, July 15, 1790: Rode to Rehoboth, where Brother Whatcoat preached, and brother Jeremiah Abel and myself spoke after him, and the people appeared somewhat affected."

Rehoboth's impact is its history, as this log cabin has only one entrance and only two quite small win-

dows. A gallery allows some seating in addition to the backless, split-log benches; a raised preaching platform constructed of crudely sawn boards is the space's main feature. Rehoboth has been treasured because of its important associations. Nevertheless, its singularity is also noteworthy as a survivor of what was once a typical ecclesiastical form across frontier America. The churches of Cades Cove, Tennessee, replaced such crude houses of worship as these, and countless similar examples were replaced when funds allowed.

The pioneer spirit of Rehoboth is remarkable, too, when compared with the architecture of other religious groups—the Moravians in North Carolina or the contemporaneous Shaker meetinghouses of New England, and especially the English Baroque and Georgian Anglicanism of tidewater churches like Saint James Episcopal Church in South Carolina, and Yeocomico Church in Virginia. These country gentlemen's parish churches represented the very Church of England that the Methodists found too stultifying and lacking in evangelical fervor. That difference, too, is reflected in the fact that Rehoboth is in what is now West Virginia. Like the Methodist Church, Virginia was split by the issue of slavery, and Monroe County became part of the breakaway state whose character is closer to the camp meeting flavor of Methodism than to Cavalier aristocracy.

Rehoboth, too, has a special symbolism in its tolerance and acceptance of other faiths. The log church was built upon land donated to the Methodists by Edward Keenan, a Roman Catholic. It was, in fact, Keenan who wrote to Francis Asbury asking him to send a preacher to Rehoboth; Keenan is buried at Rehoboth.

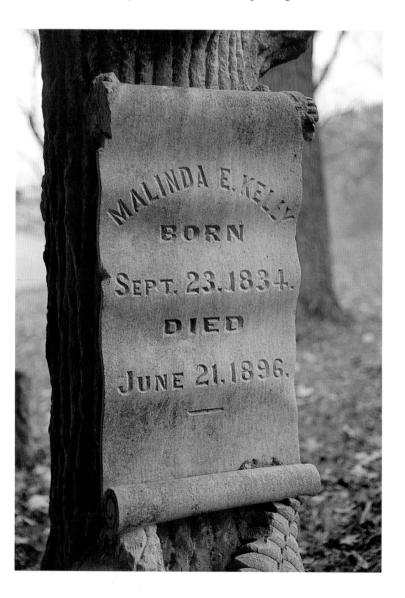

THE SCOTCH-IRISH WERE among the largest group of settlers in early West Virginia, as Melinda Kelly's grave reminds us.

Star Island Meeting House,
ISLES OF SHOALS, NEW HAMPSHIRE

Nine miles out to sea, as the seagull flies, does not seem very far. Yet, the Isles of Shoals seem very distant indeed. Barren, glacial outcrops with little vegetation under a northern sky, as if Vikings had floated a minor Scandinavian archipelago west and abandoned it. The meetinghouse that stands on the crown of Star Island is both a navigational landmark and a lookout from which to scan the horizon for ocean-borne marauders.

If the Norsemen did stop here, it no doubt reminded them too much of home, but Iberian fisherman were here soon after explorers discovered these coasts (John Smith named the islands after himself in 1614), and English fisherman were processing fish on the islands while their Pilgrim brethren were farming at Plymouth. A small group of Norwegian fishermen came in the nineteenth century (best remembered for a 1873 double homicide written about first by islands' resident Celia Thaxter and then recently by Anita Shreve in *The Weight of Water*). But despite the quality of the cod caught here, life on the islands must have been hardscrabble, even desperate. A small cemetery near the church contains the three little daughters of the minister, all of whom died of diphtheria within a few days of each other; eleven years earlier, the village's teacher was washed out to sea by a wave.

Star Island's strategic importance near Portsmouth made it a military target: a fort built here in 1652 was dismantled during the Revolutionary War to keep its guns out of the hands of the British (the inhabitants were moved to the mainland, never to return), and there was radar here in World War II. But it was the discovery of the islands by artists and vacationers that saved the islands. Artists like Thaxter, Childe Hassam, and William

THAT THIS IS THE THIRD church on this site and that its walls are two-feet thick says much about the North Atlantic storms that batter this former fishing village. The chapel has never been electrified.

THE CHAPEL NOW SERVES as a summer conference center, but the sea remains an inescapable presence. It is hard to imagine people living here in the winter—and rowing nine miles to shore as the fishermen once did.

Morris Hunt, and literary visitors like Nathaniel Hawthorne, John Greenleaf Whittier, and Harriet Beecher Stowe often stayed at one of the hotels. The chief remnant of that era is the Oceanic Hotel, now home to the Star Island Conference Center.

On summer evenings, conferees carry candles up to the nonelectrified chapel. But the meetinghouse—the third on the site—is a remnant of Star Island in 1800, when it was built to serve the island's 120 people. Nearby is the grave of Josiah Stevens, who was sent here by the Society for the Propagation of the Gospel Among the Indians, but the church was built by another cleric, Jedidiah Morse. With funds solicited from mainland churches, Morse erected two-foot-thick stone walls so that the church would survive the weather and the villagers would not burn it for fuel, as had happened to the 1720 church, itself constructed of timbers from a wrecked Spanish ship.

As the literal center of village life, the church also served as school and town hall, as well as for the drying of fish. The interior burned in 1826, and the steeple blew down sixty-two years later. Poet and carpenter Oscar Laighton fashioned an exact duplicate of the old, placing the 1852 weathervane back on top; the new bell of 1892 calls worshipers still. The inside of the thirty-six- by twenty-four-foot meetinghouse is as simple as the lives it served, while the ever-present sea is visible out the windows.

The church was originally painted lighthouse white, but now the granite has reclaimed its mottled patina. In her book on the murders, Celia Thaxter wrote of the Isles of Shoals' own cured cod called dubfish. Her description of the cod as being the "color of brown sherry walls" could equally apply to the stones of the meetinghouse.

THE STAR ISLAND CHAPEL could easily serve as a lighthouse; its steeple, topped with a fish weathervane, is the most prominent landmark on the island.

Yeocomico Church,

TUCKER HILL, VIRGINIA

THERE ARE NOT MANY 300-year-old churches in America, and Yeocomico survives in part because Tidewater churches served plantations rather than towns, and its setting is still thoroughly rural. The wicket door, the Tudor age's answer to weatherproofing, is the only one in America.

George Washington's mother and Robert E. Lee's great-grandfather were both communicants at Yeocomico Church, although such rich associations are naturally to be expected in the Virginia Tidewater. What is surprising, however, is how little the church and the setting seem to have changed in three hundred years. This was plantation country, and this little brick church is at a crossroads, not in a town. Even today rural and underdeveloped Westmoreland County seems a throwback to the times when the Carters, the Lees, and other planters shipped their tobacco directly to England from their own landings along the Potomac and Rappahannock Rivers.

Reflecting the Low Church sentiments of Anglicans in colonial times, Yeocomico takes its name from a river nearby rather than that of a saint (although the parish, Cople, honors that of one back in Bedfordshire). It would be convenient to lean on its reflected history and its relative antiquity (1703 is old for an American church, and it replaced one erected in 1655), but Yeocomico is so unusual as to defy categorization. Not only does the church reflect the paradoxes of southern Cavalier culture, but it also mystifies architectural historians.

Colonists built what they had known back home, yet Yeocomico is both a throwback to the medieval parish churches of the unchanging English countryside and a more sophisticated harbinger of the classically inspired Georgian style. Built of bricks fired on the site, Yeocomico has certain features—a hint of tracery, lamb's-tongue moldings, blocky altar table, and even the distinctive "kick" eaves—that are Jacobean, while the octagonal font and the T-shaped plan suggest the Georgian fascination with geometry. Yeocomico has been altered and restored so many

THE TEN COMMANDMENTS

I
I am the Lord thy God: Thou shalt have
none other gods but me.

II
Thou shalt not make to thyself any grav-
en image, nor the likeness of any thing that is
in heaven above, or in the earth beneath,
or in the water under the earth;thou shalt
not bow down to them,nor worship them.

III
Thou shalt not take the Name of the Lord
thy God in vain.

IV
Remember that thou keep holy the Sabbath-day.

V
Honour thy father and thy mother.

VI
Thou shalt do no murder.

VII
Thou shalt not commit adultery.

VIII
Thou shalt not steal.

IX
Thou shalt not bear false witness against
thy neighbour.

X
Thou shalt not covet.

SUMMARY OF THE LAW

Thou shalt love the Lord thy God with
all thy heart, and with all thy soul, and
with all thy mind. This is the first and
great commandment. And the second is
like unto it; Thou shalt love thy neighbour
as thyself. On these two commandments
hang all the Law and the Prophets.

times that its exact history may never be known. The unparallel walls (there's not a right angle anywhere) and America's only Tudor-style wicket door (a door within a door to keep out the weather) infer that memory won over ambition here.

Yeocomico wears its age well, but it is incredible that the church survives at all. Following disestablishment of the Church of England in Virginia after the Revolution, the church was used as a schoolhouse and a barn. During the War of 1812, American soldiers destroyed much of the interior and used the altar table and font for decidedly nonecclesiastical purposes (one soldier, William Rogers of Princeton, New Jersey, returned a few years later to repair the damage). Confederate Home Guards were billeted here during the War Between the States. In 1906, in celebration of the church's putative bicentennial, Yeocomico was rather enthusiastically restored; renovations followed in the 1920s, 1930s, and 1950s (the church was not electrified until 1947). The brick floors were installed in 1820, the pews in 1873, and the

YEOCOMICO IS AN IDIOSYNCRATIC design with an unusually complicated building history. But most reassuringly, it remains a parish church and a tangible link to a rich past.

pulpit in 1928; much of the woodwork is late nineteenth century, while brick walls reflect the hands of many masons over time.

The element that perhaps best expresses the paradoxical crudeness and elegance of Yeocomico Church is its baptismal font. Dating to about 1740, the octagonal marble bowl was bought in London and represented the latest fashion. The base, on the other hand, is serviceable sandstone and no doubt locally made.

Antioch Baptist Church,

PERRY COUNTY, ALABAMA

*I*n the 1930s, writer James Agee and photographer Walker Evans documented the lives of three Alabama sharecropping families. Their subsequent classic book, *Let Us Now Praise Famous Men*, gave the area a certain notoriety as one of the poorest places in a country that had been mired in the Great Depression. But Hale County has been poor for a very long time; the agrarian wealth of this once-fertile region disappeared with the Civil War and Reconstruction. Interstates, industry, and prosperity have continued to bypass this predominantly black community. Life here revolves around hard work, neighbors and family, and the church.

Things have changed dramatically if quietly since 1993 when Auburn University's school of architecture opened its Rural Studio in Newbern. Fifteen to twenty students live in Hale County, where their work consists of erecting housing and assisting in various civic projects. Under the direction of Dennis Ruth and the late Samuel Mockbee, young designers have built houses, a market, a community center, a clubhouse, a baseball field, and churches. Mockbee, Ruth recalls, "believed and honored the thought that architecture should serve the commonplace, expressing its spirit and enabling its culture."

Mockbee, sometimes called "architecture's conscience," challenged his students to create innovative but inexpensive structures without abandoning their aesthetic principles. The result has been some astounding works of architecture that are both respectful of the local traditions and avant-garde. Working with their clients, the students have constructed buildings out of hay bales, bottles, license plates, street signs, carpet tiles, and cardboard. Yancey Chapel is made of discarded tires; the walls of Mason's Bend Community Center are composed of rammed earth and eighty recycled Chevrolet Caprice windshields.

When architecture students renovated the baseball field in Mason's Bend, one of the players asked the Rural Studio if they might help with repairs to his church in nearby Perry County. Antioch Baptist had major structural problems, and as the church was without either baptistry or bathroom, its small membership was dwindling.

THE NEW CHURCH NOT ONLY has the furniture from the old church, but also sits on the same site, and worshippers can look out upon the graves of their families.

A thesis studio—Jared Fulton, Marion McElroy, Gabe Michaud, Bill Nauck, and Professor Andrew Freear—took on the church. While they were unable to save the 1907 frame structure, they salvaged corrugated metal, flooring and joists, and paneling from it, along with additional wood from the abandoned Oak Grove Baptist Church down the road, as well as cinder blocks from dorms at Auburn. During construction, the team built a small temporary chapel for use by the fifteen-member congregation.

Antioch may have been small and isolated, but it had been a spiritual home for many black Baptists; some of its people have worshiped here for more than half a century. Now their legacy has been assured by a new sanctuary, in the same place and of the same materials as the old one. The windows at eye-level with the cemetery maintain that connection, while the new baptistry means that churchgoers do not have to walk out to Payne Lake to perform their most important sacrament. The simple, recycled materials have been used in a dramatic way: the design is contemporary, yet it captures that Southern spirit of this place that Sambo Mockbee loved so much.

Saint Wenceslaus Church,

SPILLVILLE, IOWA

SPILLVILLE, IOWA, WILL BE forever linked with the name of the great Romantic composer Antonin Dvořák, who spent the summer of 1893 in this small Czech community.

Saint Wenceslaus Church overlooks the Turkey River in the northeastern Iowa village of Spillville. The topography is not flat, but gently rolling, much as depicted in the landscapes by Iowan Grant Wood. The rich loam of Winneshiek County—some of the Midwest's best farmland—was especially attractive to immigrants. The county seat of Decorah was an important center of Norwegian culture, but the area along the river was home to some of Iowa's earliest Czech settlers. Czech and German speakers from the Bohemian and Moravian parts of the Austro-Hungarian Empire found a countryside much like that they had left behind.

Tradition holds that Saint Wenceslaus is modeled after the cathedral of Saint Barbara's in Kutná Hora, although it was named for the Czechs' patron saint. This stone church could be a stand-in for many Roman Catholic churches erected by Germans and central Europeans throughout the old Midwest. Nevertheless, Spillville's church is an unusually substantial edifice for a town of a few hundred families. The tower was no doubt meant to be taller and constructed of stone, but everything else about the cruciform church is imposing: pointed-arch windows, round transepts, polygonal apse. Eight ministeeples (complete with louvered belfries, squared-domed roofs, and crosses) atop the apse and transept buttresses create a picturesque secondary skyline. Interior decoration is limited to the chancel, almost suggesting that the church's fine masonry left little in the budget for statuary and painting.

What really sets Spillville and its church apart is the association with Antonín Dvořák, who spent a summer here in 1893. The world-famous Czech composer had come to New York to head up a music con-

servatory, where he learned much about new forms of music from African-American students at the school. His symphony, *From the New World*, clearly owes a debt to southern spirituals ("In the Negro melodies of America," Dvořák wrote, "I discovered all that is needed for a great and noble school of music.") One of his Prague pupils, Josef Kovarik, was from Spillville and convinced Dvořák to take his family to Iowa. ("Master," he argued, "the population is 350 people and they are all Bohemian—except for one German, one Swiss, and one Norwegian.") So, Dvořák took his wife and six children on the train to Calmar, Iowa, via Philadelphia, Chicago, and Dubuque.

One of the attractions of Spillville spelled out by Kovarik was that Saint Wenceslaus Church had a good organ—a Pfeffer installed in 1876. Throughout the summer, Dvořák played the organ for Sunday services. But the composer's great joy was exploring the pleasant countryside, often carrying both violin and fishing pole. After the fast pace of New York, listening to the birds and farm animals of Spillville proved just the right sort of inspiration. Building upon the song of a tanager, Dvořák composed his string quartet known as the "American," and it had its first performance in Spillville: Dvořák played the violin and three members of the Kovarik family provided second violin, viola, and cello.

Spillville is the same size as it was when the Dvořáks were in residence. But the composer's visit has forever marked Spillville and probably saved Saint Wenceslaus as a treasured church among hundreds of immigrant churches in our heartland.

THE SUBSTANTIAL STONE CHURCH was the center of life in Spillville and it had a good organ that Dvořák played every Sunday. The visiting Dvořáks felt very much at home in a place that looked, felt, and sounded like Czechoslovakia.

DVOŘÁK WROTE HIS "Symphony from the New World" while teaching in New York, but it was in Iowa that he was inspired to write the sublime string quartet known as the "American."

Assumption of the Blessed Virgin Mary Church,

RANCHO BARONA, CALIFORNIA

THE CATHOLIC CHURCH AT the Rancho Barona Indian Reservation is a respectful nod to the Spanish mission tradition in California. Yet, it was designed by a Quaker modernist architect who had trained with Frank Lloyd Wright.

The Assumption of the Blessed Virgin Mary Church is one of the least-known works by one of California's most admired architects. Irving Gill came to San Diego from Chicago in 1893 after an apprenticeship with Louis Sullivan and Frank Lloyd Wright. Although the young designer was attracted to southern California for its salubrious climate, he embraced its culture, finding inspiration in both the Spanish tradition and the relaxed atmosphere of the West Coast. Gill abandoned the styles he learned "Back East" and developed a personal language that was at once rooted in the West's romantic history and supremely modern.

Irving Gill is revered as one of America's great modern architects, although during his lifetime his reductive, almost Cubist forms were more appreciated by the European avant-garde than by his fellow countrymen. His masterpiece, the Walter L. Dodge House in West Hollywood (1914–16), had the plain blocky forms of the adobe builders, along with patios and arcades from the missions. But its forms and masses were abstract, reduced to basic fundamentals. As Gill wrote, "If we, the architects of the West, wish to do great and lasting work, we must dare to be simple" and to rely not upon stylistic flourishes but upon the "source of all architectural strength—the straight line, the arch, the cube and the circle."

It is not hard to discern the spirit of the Spanish missions in Gill's flat roofs and plain facades. But much of Gill's work addressed the issue of low-cost, high-quality housing, and this is where the simple forms of the pueblo were married to the modern material of concrete. True to his Quaker upbringing, Gill was concerned with the plight of the workers and the underprivileged. As early as 1913 he designed model barracks for migrant workers at a cement factory.

Housing was Gill's real love, but he was also an important church designer. His Catholic, Christian Scientist, Episcopal, and African Methodist churches were light on ornament and popularly perceived as similar to nearby mission architecture. Assumption was Gill's last church, and it exemplifies the melding of his artistic beliefs and social concerns.

In 1932 the federal government commissioned Gill to design a church and thirty houses for a group of Indians who had been displaced from their homes by the construction of a reservoir. Gill moved to the Rancho Barona Indian Reservation to train the Indians to build their own houses, but only a dozen houses were erected. His argument for clustered housing in the native tradition was rejected as socialistic, so that the church assumed an even greater role in creating a sense of community.

If there was a mission source at Barona, it would be rural New Mexico rather than metropolitan California. The church was later altered by the addition of a second bell tower—added to make the facade symmetrical and more in keeping with general notions of an early mission. Yet the timeless quality of the stark white church remains. For despite his modernist reputation, Irving Gill tapped age-old wisdom; he knew that simplest was best. In deliberately aiming for the modest, the timeless, and the primitive, Gill achieved greatness that transcended considerations of style.

AS WITH SO MANY MISSIONS of the Southwest, this 1932 church is a combination of Spanish and Native-American influences.

Faith Chapel,

JEKYLL ISLAND, GEORGIA

*I*t is hard to believe that the architect of Faith Chapel is not known, for this 1904 shingled church is the epitome of a private chapel in a turn-of-the-twentieth-century resort for the very rich. Faced with an old photograph of the chapel framed by palm trees, one could be excused for identifying this as a piece of England planted in British India. Indeed, there is much influence of the Arts and Crafts movement here: the heavy wrought-iron door hinges, the self-conscious rusticity of the interior, and the picturesque quality of the setting. Faith Chapel could be attributed to any of a number of the leading New York architects, but the lack of an attribution of an undoubtedly famous designer does not detract from the church's charm.

Faith Chapel is the center of a demiparadise, for the ideal climate of Jekyll Island offered Gilded Age tycoons a felicitous private place to spend winters along the coast. Vanderbilts, Astors, and Pulitzers arrived on the island in the late 1880s; Morgans, Rockefellers, Macys, Goulds, and Goodyears built cottages here. A consortium, calling themselves the Jekyll Island Club—the most exclusive club in the country—bought the island from the duBignon family, refugee French royalists. The original owner of the island was William Horton, a confederate of James Oglethorpe in his fight against the Spanish for control of this part of the Atlantic Coast.

This Sea Islands house of worship served the club members until the islands were evacuated during World War II. Although nominally nondenominational, a string of vacationing Episcopal priests were on hand to conduct services, while waiters from the rambling Jekyll Island Hotel made up the choir. In 1947 the state bought the island and restored the

REMINISCENT OF A SHINGLED cottage at a late nineteenth-century seaside resort, this chapel ministered to the Jekyll Island winter colony of some of Americas wealthiest families.

LOUIS COMFORT TIFFANY designed a window at Faith Chapel, but Maitland Armstrong, a Tiffany student, created *The Adoration of the Christ Child* behind the altar.

badly deteriorated church in the 1990s. Faith Chapel is now a popular wedding spot, and it is easy to understand why.

With its corner bell tower and shingled spire, Faith is an American descendant of an English country church. In medieval fashion, carved gargoyles jut out from the corners of the tower just below the eaves, while similar grotesques adorn timbering in the nave (local legend holds that the tower gargoyles are replicas of some at Notre-Dame in Paris, but the fashion is equally English). More to the point, the carving was a creative outlet for the architect and his craftsmen. These carvings, as well as the arch separating nave from chancel, recall the handsome and beloved New England libraries of H. H. Richardson.

The shingled nave with its score of plain pine pews and exposed trusses offers the beauty of simplicity. Nevertheless, wedding parties and devotees of Faith Chapel would say the glory of this little church is its two magnificent stained-glass windows. Louis Comfort Tiffany's *David* and Maitland Armstrong's *Adoration of the Christ Child* show the sometime partners' mastery of opalescent Art Nouveau glass. Less well known than his mentor, Armstrong was trained as a lawyer, turned to painting, and then to glass; as an aspiring artist in Paris he roomed with sculptor Augustus Saint-Gaudens and was friends with architect Stanford White and painter John La Farge. Tiffany's *David set Singers before the Lord* was given in honor of Jekyll Island Club president Frederick Bourne, head of—amusingly—the Singer Sewing Machine Company.

Bethabara Moravian Church,
WINSTON-SALEM, NORTH CAROLINA

When Augustus Spangenberg led a group of fifteen men from the Lehigh Valley of Pennsylvania to piedmont North Carolina in the autumn of 1753, he was continuing a spiritual journey begun in central Europe three centuries before. Bishop Spangenberg's group was the Unity of Brethren, more popularly known as the Moravians in honor of their homeland. One of the oldest of Protestant groups, the German-speaking Moravians barely survived the upheavals of the Reformation. When the Brethren reorganized in Saxony in the early eighteenth century, they pledged themselves to carry their peace-loving, communitarian message to the New World, particularly to the Native Americans.

The war between the Spanish and the English for the control of the Georgia coast drove the Moravians from their first American mainland settlement in

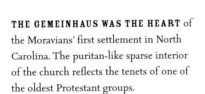

THE GEMEINHAUS WAS THE HEART of the Moravians' first settlement in North Carolina. The puritan-like sparse interior of the church reflects the tenets of one of the oldest Protestant groups.

BETHABARA IS UNUSUAL in that it was designed from the first to be church, school, and parsonage. The tall and efficient tile stove is a central European form.

Savannah to Bethlehem, Pennsylvania. The Moravians were extremely literate (they had their own presses and published their own Bibles); they also had very definite ideas about town planning as a mirror of their sense of the universe. Every aspect of town life was inextricably interwoven with the ecclesiastical one, so when growth threatened to upset the utopian ideal balance of agriculture, industry, and church life, the Moravians preferred to start a new settlement.

Settling in the Carolina hills was both spiritual and practical. Thus, when the new settlement at Bethabara grew to a certain size in a few years, another community—Bethania—was established, and then,

in 1766, Salem. Although neither Salem nor Bethabara remained rural, they survive as restored villages. The Bethabara congregation moved to a new building nearby some years ago, but the church of the first North Carolina settlement remains very much as it was when built by the Moravians.

Constructed in 1788, the Gemeinhaus served as both church and community center, with the minister living in one half of the building (the broken roofline marks the separation; the ministers also got two chimneys). This meeting place–church–school reflects the sophisticated design of the Moravian communities: both the designer, Frederick William Marshall, and the master mason, Abraham Loesch,

are known, and they were undoubtedly sent south from the home church in Bethlehem. Like so many buildings of immigrants, this reflects the styles that the newcomers knew back home. The bell-cast shape of the roof, the octagonal bell tower, and even the brickwork would not be out of place in a village in the Czech Republic.

But it is inside the church that one really feels transported back to the spirit of Protestant dissenters, back to the worlds of Jan Hus and Martin Luther protesting the splendors of Roman Catholicism. The church itself, or *Saal*, is an exceedingly plain room. Like their cemeteries, Moravians segregated their worshipers by gender, and, as in their careful town planning, there are rules for stratified seating—by age, marital status, or whether you might be an outsider or a slave. The stark bareboned quality is reinforced by backless benches, the total lack of ornamentation, and the tall roundarched windows with their clear panes—which, if not admitting the light of reason, do at least avoid the conceits of color.

Wheelock Mission
Presbyterian Church,

MCCURTAIN COUNTY, OKLAHOMA

The life and fate of a church is often bound up with one or two amazingly strong people. Wheelock Church is a memorial to a most remarkable churchman, but he also stands as the epitome of so many other men of the cloth who took religion to the Indians. The oldest church building in Oklahoma is a testament to Alfred Wright's faith, a servant of God who gave thirty-three of his seventy-five years to the Choctaw Tribe. His grave in the little cemetery nearby refers to him as "Man, Minister, Physician, Translator, Christian."

Born in Connecticut, Wright was a graduate of Williams College, where the American Board for the Commissions for Foreign Missions was founded. After seminary, he joined the American Board in its mission to the Choctaw Tribe in Mississippi. When the Choctaws were forcibly "removed" to the west in 1832, Wright and his wife, Harriet, traveled the Trail of Tears with their flock. Upon their arrival, Wright led his small band of survivors in the first Presbyterian service in what was Indian Territory.

A log church was soon built, but the Wrights' major effort was schooling for the Indians. Mrs. Wright taught Choctaw children and in 1839 established Wheelock Academy, a boarding school for girls. Wheelock (named for Eleazar Wheelock, founder of Dartmouth College, which itself started as a school for Indians) was the model for all subsequent Choctaw education and served students until the 1950s. Meanwhile, Reverend Wright was the only trained physician around and treated dozens of patients a day, healing and burying members of the tribe during cholera and typhoid epidemics. He supervised the mission's five outlying preaching stations, and he also translated the Bible into Choctaw.

The Choctaw wanted a more permanent church that

THE CENTER OF MISSIONARY activity among the Choctaw Tribe, Wheelock is the oldest church building in Oklahoma.

THE FOUNDER OF WHEELOCK, Alfred Wright, was a preacher and a doctor, and he translated the Bible into Choctaw.

symbolized their achievements in the West, so the "Old Stone Church" was built in 1846. Constructed of locally quarried limestone (the walls are twenty inches thick) with one piece of granite—a block over the door inscribed "Jehovah Jireh" (the Lord Will Provide), it is a preaching box of the kind built by countless Protestant denominations settling the American hinterlands: simple, functional, and dignified. Wheelock is a New England meetinghouse erected by transplanted New Englanders.

When Alfred Wright died in 1853, he was succeeded by John Edwards, a graduate of Princeton and a descendant of the Puritan divine Jonathan Edwards. Like his sponsoring organization, Edwards was

antislavery and was forced to flee Wheelock at the outbreak of the War Between the States. Then in 1869 the school burned down and the church was reduced to just its walls. But as fate would have it, Edwards returned to the mission in 1884, rebuilt the school, and fixed up the church. Eventually, the Presbyterian Church purchased Wheelock and rededicated it as a memorial to Wright and missionary efforts among the Indians.

In his first sermon in the West, Alfred Wright has said: "It is here, I trust, that my labors will glorify His name." Fittingly, it was one of Wright's parishioners and chief of the Choctaw Nation who suggested that the Indian Territory be called Oklahoma.

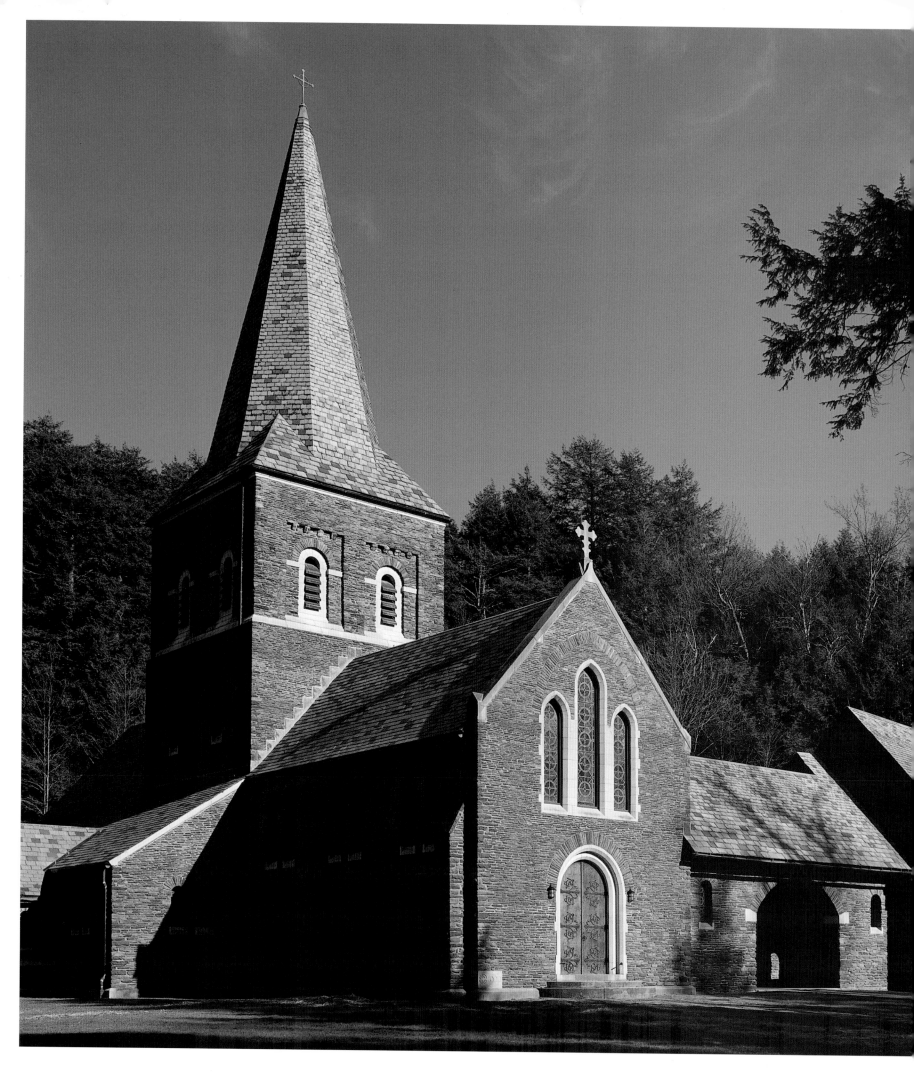

Saint James' Church,

LAKE DELAWARE, NEW YORK

Saint James' Church sits alongside the Little Delaware River in the western Catskill Mountains, something of a surprise for the traveler on the Andes-Delhi road. This is dairy farming and vacation country, so one does not expect to find a near-perfect Romanesque church. Saint James' was not imported stone by stone from Europe by some wealthy robber baron. Rather, this romantic and evocative jewel is the work of one of America's greatest ecclesiastical architects. Saint James' may not be on the beaten path to anywhere, but it is nonetheless a treasure, a work of art, a masterpiece in every sense.

The patrons of the church were the Gerry family (descendants of James Madison's vice president, the lawmaker eponymously remembered for the gerrymander), who summered at their horse farm near the village of Bovina in the late nineteenth century. The family drove to Saint John's Church seven miles away in Delhi, and on one exasperating morning Commodore Elbridge Gerry is reputed to have remarked, "I wish there were a church here, then perhaps you children could get to Sunday School on time." Sunday school instruction notwithstanding, Gerry's daughters had a great influence in local Episcopal-church life: Mabel began a mission here in 1914, and Angelica built the church eight years later.

For Miss Angelica the choice of an architect was easy: Boston Gothicist Ralph Adams Cram, designer of such churches as Saint Thomas' and the Cathedral

REMINISCENT OF A MEDIEVAL monastery along a pilgrimage road, Saint James' seems to have occupied its site for almost a thousand years.

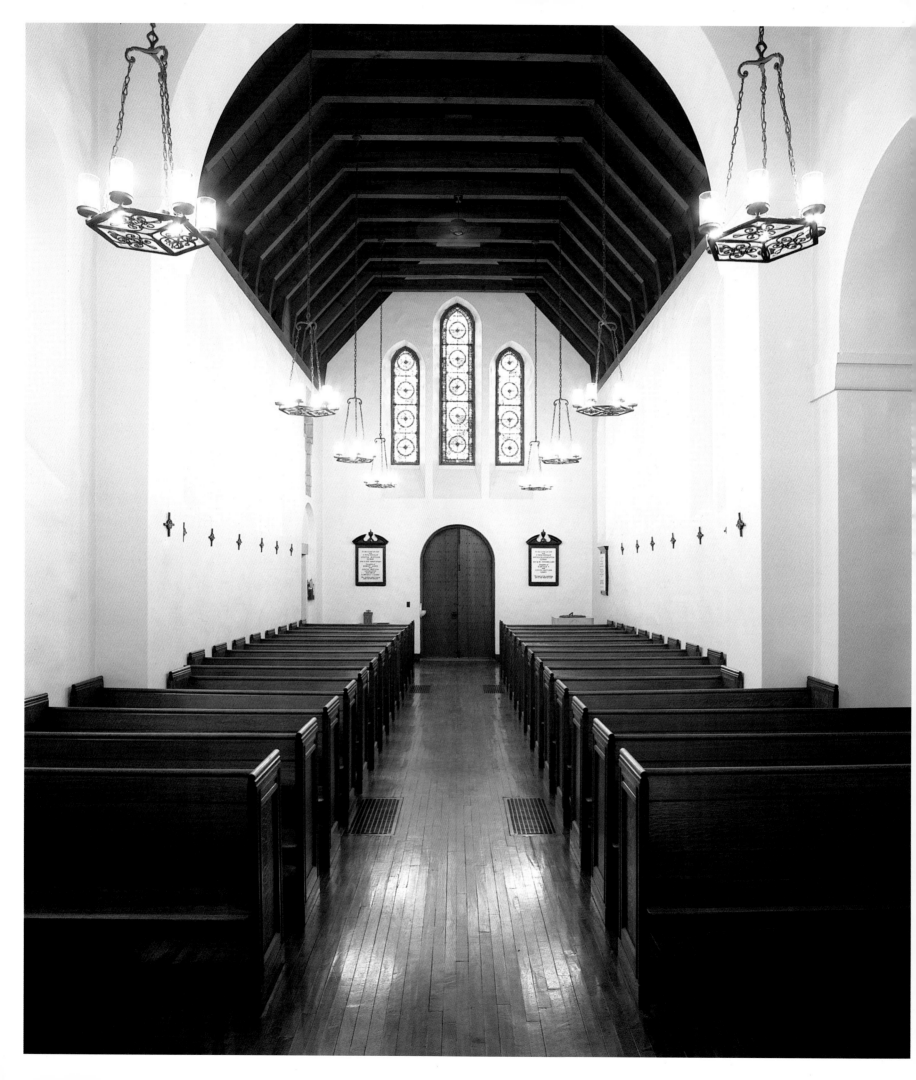

RALPH ADAMS CRAM, the designer of Saint James', was the leading ecclesiastical architect of his day. Famous for colleges and cathedrals, his smaller parish churches are among his most successful works.

in the machine but through the application of careful handwork.

Cram's philosophical positions were virtually obliterated by the advent of European Modernism in the United States. The Princeton University Chapel is, ironically, contemporary with Walter Gropius's revolutionary design school, the Bauhaus. Nevertheless, Cram was a hugely successful architect, with an enormous output of significant work, including skyscrapers. Yet his small churches are perhaps the best expression of his design principles.

For Saint James', Cram employed the more rural Romanesque, Gothic being something of an urban style (although he applied a veneer of age by including later Gothic lancets and a brooch spire, as if Saint James' had been built over several centuries). But ultimately, style was less important to Cram than proportion, massing, and structural expression; craftsmanship was more important than abundant detail.

The nave of Saint James' comprises plaster walls and simple framing. Employing many of the great craftsmen whom Cram patronized, decoration is centered on the chancel, specifically the altar. Here, Boston's finest wood-carver, Johannes Kirchmayer, included Miss Angelica's Airedale among the worshipful Magi. The Lady Chapel is smaller and more jewellike, with a sparkling blue and gold color scheme and a thirteenth-century Florentine triptych featuring the Enthronement of Mary.

The genius of Saint James' is its powerful massing. It recalls Romanesque chapels along the pilgrimage roads in France and Spain to Saint James the Great's burial place in Compostela, or the monastery chapels that kept Christianity alive in the Celtic fringes of Britain (not to mention Iffley Church in Oxfordshire, a favorite English Romanesque source for Cram). With its Indiana limestone, brown shale gathered from local fences, and slate roofs, Saint James' offers a sense of solidity and permanence. It is the perfect country church.

Church of Saint John the Divine in Manhattan. But Cram was more than just a church designer—he was campus architect for schools such as Princeton, MIT, and Wellesley. Most of all, he was the leading apologist for a revivified medievalism: through his writings, buildings, and personality he advocated a Modern Gothic with pre-Reformation roots but without Victorian theatricality. Cram was a firm believer in the Arts and Crafts ethic espoused by William Morris, that redemption could be found not

INTERIOR DECORATION IS LIMITED to the windows and the altars. Donor Angelica Gerry insisted that carver Johannes Kirchmayer include her Airedale in the Adoration scene at the main altar.

ARCHITECT CRAM BELIEVED IN strong, simple masses with limited exterior embellishment, yet he hired the best craftsmen to re-create elaborate medieval metalwork for his church doorways.

Saint Paul's Lutheran Church,

SERBIN, TEXAS

*I*n many ways the painted church at Serbin seems a lot like that at Praha fifty miles to the south. Both were built by central European refugees in search of freedom and cheap land, they were the centers of their respective cultures, and each experienced decline of their onetime thriving communities with the construction of a railroad town nearby. Here, too, are marbleized wooden columns and gilded details, and the similar heavenly blue color scheme of the ceiling.

Saint Paul's in Serbin, nevertheless, is different from Praha and most of the Roman Catholic painted churches of East Texas. The celestial ceiling is flat, and the columns painted to look like veined stone are square; there is much less in the way of carved decoration, and the whole speaks of Reformation restraint rather than an exuberant and militant Catholicism. The remarkable two-story pulpit is the focus of worship here, for this is a church where the Word predominated. A prominent balcony wraps around three sides, for worshipers were divided—men upstairs, women and children downstairs—until as late as World War II.

LIKE A EUCHARISTIC LAMP, this Texas church kept alive the cultural flame of the Wendish-speaking Lutherans who came here from Germany in search of religious and linguistic freedom.

THE CEILINGS WERE PAINTED heavenly blue, the square columns marbleized, and highlights gilded in 1906, but the main focus of Saint Paul's is the two-story pulpit. As conservative Lutherans, their service was centered on the Word. The last Wendish sermon was delivered from the pulpit in 1921.

Some Wends went to Australia and others went to Texas; the largest group left Hamburg and sailed to Galveston in 1854. Half a thousand faithful were led by Pastor Johan Kilian, a Leipzig-trained theologian, known as the Moses of the Sorbs. Kilian had translated Luther, and he wrote prayers, tracts, and hymns in Wendish; he preached his Sunday sermons in Wendish, German, and English. Kilian led his flock to what is now Lee County in 1855, where he set aside ninety-five acres for a church and a Lutheran school.

Serbin was to be the center of Wendish culture in America, and the school lasted until 1971. As the Wends prospered (they were corn and cotton growers), they colonized other parts of Texas. German was a second language for the Sorbs and they easily joined with the large numbers of German settlers in Texas. Eventually, the very language that the Wends had moved to the New World to preserve died out. The last service in Wendish was in 1921, about the time the *Deutsches Volksblatt* in the county seat of Giddings ceased running a column in Sorbian.

Saint Paul's got its organ in 1904, and two years later the church interior was painted. That time was probably the zenith of Wendish culture in Texas, when the language was strong and the community wealthy enough to embellish their church in memory of the homeland. The Texas Wendish Historical Society was founded when the school closed, and every year a Wendish Fest—Witajc e K'nam—keeps the Sorbian legacy alive.

Completed in 1871, Saint Paul's is a rectangular preaching box: there are tall pointed windows and a simple belfry; the roughcast walls have a peasant solidity to them. Serbin is the mother church of a little-known ethnic group from Germany known as the Wends. The Wends (or Sorbs as they call themselves) have their own Slavonic tongue; they endured persecution in Saxony and Brandenburg for more than a thousand years. Prussian insistence that they speak German and practice a less-conservative reformed Lutheranism finally drove many Wends to emigrate in the mid-nineteenth century.

Herr erhebe Dich in Deiner Kraft so wollen wir singen und loben Deine Macht. Ps. 21,14

THE NORTH GERMAN AUSTERITY of the exterior gives little hint to the richness within, although thirty-five years separates the two—during which time the immigrants had become successful farmers.

Trinity Church,

BROOKLYN, CONNECTICUT

Connecticut is much more than just another segment of the megalopolis that sprawls from Virginia to north of Boston, although one may hold images of a number of gritty factory cities like Bridgeport, New Britain, and Waterbury. There are parts of the state that are quite rural and areas where farming still dominates the landscape. Windham County, tucked up against the borders of Rhode Island and Massachusetts, is Connecticut's least populated and the least spoiled. And set among its rolling farmland and woodlots is a gem of a church that is so special in part because it is so unexpected.

Trinity Church in Brooklyn also has a most unusual history. That Trinity is the oldest church in the first diocese of a post-Revolutionary (hence "Protestant") Episcopal Church is almost a minor point compared to the fascinating tale of why it was built and by whom. The protagonists alone, Godfrey Malbone and Israel Putnam, tell us much about architecture and religion in colonial New England.

Putnam was the farmer-patriot who later fought on the side of George Washington against the British, and he was a pillar of the Congregational Church. Malbone was an English-educated Royalist from Newport, Rhode Island, whose father sent him to manage a considerable landholding in Brooklyn. Putnam wanted to replace the town's 1734 meeting-house, but Malbone refused to contribute. Instead, Malbone erected an Anglican church far from the village, employing his slaves for labor.

Both churches were completed in 1771. Putnam's was a big boxy New England meetinghouse. Trinity, on the other hand, was as high style as Malbone's design abilities and pockets would allow. Unlike this

THIS FRONTIER CHURCH REFLECTS the contemporary styles of Newport and London, as its patron was familiar with both. Trinity came about because one wealthy Anglican refused to support the building of a Congregational meetinghouse.

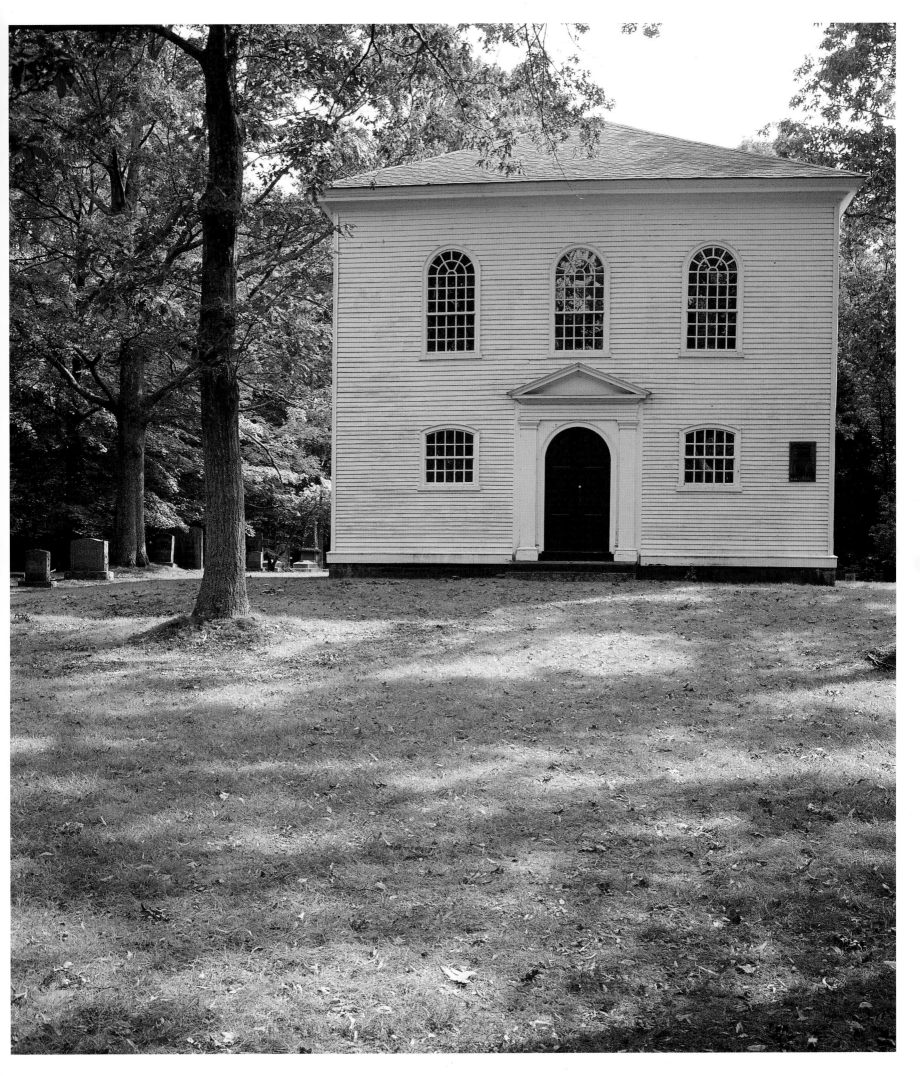

Connecticut backwater, Newport was one of the leading architectural centers of the Colonies; it even boasted a wealthy gentleman who has been called America's first architect. For Peter Harrison, architecture was an avocation, yet he created some of our first monumental civic structures. Malbone knew Harrison, and as Harrison relied upon pattern books by English architects, it was only natural that Malbone would replicate Harrison's work in Connecticut (imitation of the canons of taste was considered not only acceptable but desirable in the eighteenth century).

Malbone's new church was named after Trinity in Newport, which was not by Harrison. The Brooklyn church echoes Harrison's larger and more magnificent King's Chapel in Boston, but it is Harrison's Touro Synagogue in Newport that is the closet model for Trinity. There are the same round-topped Venetian windows (borrowed from James Gibbs's influential Book of Architecture), the regionally unexpected nearly flat roof, and most of all the simple, cubic forms that expressed the ideals of the Renaissance-inspired English Georgian. Proportion and elegance were more important than denomination for the eighteenth-century church designer with any architectural pretensions.

In keeping with the more "Protestant" Anglicanism of the time, Trinity Church is an open preaching space with box pews and a balcony around three sides. The same can be said of Harrison's Sephardic house of worship as well. The difference is that daydreamers in Brooklyn could look out upon a much wilder landscape. The delightful irony of this ecumenism has a further reflection in Brooklyn. Israel Putnam's son married Godfrey Malbone's daughter and became a senior warden at Trinity. Later, when the Episcopalians erected a new Trinity, they relocated to town and built right across from Putnam's meetinghouse.

ALTHOUGH SEEMINGLY PLAIN, Trinity Church was designed following the latest London pattern books, and with a sophisticated eye toward proportional relationships.

THE TRINITY CEMETERY CONTAINS graves from the Revolutionary War up to the present, so stones run the gamut of styles, from flat slates carved with seraphim and urns to Victorian crosses and flat military plaques.

The Monastery of Christ in the Desert,

ABIQUIU, NEW MEXICO

O ne expects a spiritual dimension at the center of a Benedictine monastery. The chapel at the Monastery of Christ in the Desert, however, represents more than just a tradition that goes back to medieval Burgundy; the adobe church also bears the legacy of Spanish Colonial missions. Yet it is also the product of a lifelong spiritual quest. Christ in the Desert is the culmination of a pilgrimage by designer George Nakashima that included India, Japan, Paris, and a concentration camp in Idaho.

Christ in the Desert, miles from the nearest highway, is home to only a score of monks and a handful of retreatants. The monastery's great virtue is the setting almost seven thousand feet up in the red-rock mountains of northwestern New Mexico. The Abiquiu region is sacred—an ancient pueblo and ruined missions are close by, a place of haunting beauty that attracted artists such as Georgia O'Keeffe.

The church has to hold up to the fierce sun, strong wind, and extreme temperatures of the Chama Canyon Wilderness. It also had to be inexpensive—it is built of adobe and hay bales reinforced with chicken wire. Above all, the chapel was not to compete with, but to be one with, the magnificent setting of massive sandstone cliffs and some of the West's most dramatic skies.

Inside the church there are half-log benches, religious vessels of local pottery, and contemporary carvings. The total effect is of utter simplicity, cloistered tranquility, denial of the material world, and a personal sense of faith. The chapel pays homage to other missions like Trampas or Acoma, but high clerestories render a much different kind of sensory experience. These windows bring the ever-changing New

BUILT INEXPENSIVELY OF ADOBE and hay bales, this Benedictine monastery in the New Mexico wilderness is one of four churches designed by George Nakashima, best known as a furniture maker.

THE CHAPEL AT CHRIST in the Desert Monastery does not try to compete with its magnificent mountain landscape, but is a part of it.

Mexico sky into the sanctuary. The altar is a simple stone table, for what furnishings could compete with the wash of light?

The elemental primacy of nature at Abiquiu is an expression of architect George Nakashima's belief that creativity must be divorced from ego; each day was another step on a spiritual journey. Nakashima was best known as a furniture maker, a craft he learned from a carpenter while in an internment camp for Japanese-Americans during World War II. Although the East certainly influenced him, the handcrafted chairs and tables he produced in his shop in New Hope, Pennsylvania, were equally informed by an enthusiasm for modern architecture.

A native of Spokane, Washington, Nakashima studied architecture at MIT and in Paris where he became a devotee of Le Corbusier. He went to Japan to work with an associate of Frank Lloyd Wright, who

ARCHITECT NAKASHIMA COMMISSIONED local artists to do the reredos, furniture, and statuary, while his plain stone altar echoes the chapel's powerful simplicity.

sent him to build a dormitory for an ashram in India. The guru, Sri Aurobindo, gave his disciple the Sanskrit name Sundarananda: one who delights in beauty. Eventually, Nakashima's spiritual search led him to Roman Catholicism, but he did not abandon the cultural lessons learned along the way.

And while Nakashima focused most of his creative energies on furniture, for him all design was generated by spiritual force. In addition to Christ in the Desert, he designed two churches in Japan and another Benedictine monastery in Mexico.

Welsh Hill Church,

CLIFFORD TOWNSHIP, PENNSYLVANIA

This white frame church in the countryside near the village of Dundaff goes by a variety of names: Welsh Hill Church, Welsh Methodist Church, Welsh Methodist Congregational Church, Welsh Hill Methodist Church, Welsh Hill Methodist Congregational Church, and the Old Welsh Church. Its official name is Bethel Congregational Tabernacle. An offspring of the First Welsh Congregational Church in Clifford, which dates to 1833, it should not be confused with the Welsh Congregational Church in nearby Forest City. But there is certainly no confusion about the ethnic origin of its builders. Preaching in English did not even begin here until 1893.

Built during the pastorate of Daniel Daniels (who served from 1850 to 1892), Welsh Hill is a slightly Victorian variant of the by now very familiar, almost generic American church building. The body of the church has three bays, marked by round-headed windows filled with colored glass; similar windows flank the entrance. A round drip molding surrounds the top of the main entrance, itself the base of a belfry, which in a rather inventive country carpenter's way looks as though it were pushed up through the roof. The belfry is octagonal, with eight arched openings and paired brackets supporting the cornice of its roof. The colored glass, the brackets, and the neo-Italianate windows are the only elements that could remotely be called high style.

Decorative embellishments aside, the Old Welsh Church could mistakenly be identified as a rural church in Colorado, Montana, California, or Georgia of the same period. It could be Presbyterian, Baptist, or Methodist; place a cross atop the belfry and it could be Catholic. The interior is filled with a slightly filtered light; there is no fancy carving, and just a

LIKE PLAIN PREACHING-BOX churches all across America, this rural northeastern Pennsylvania example reflects the hard-working, God-fearing Protestant immigrants from Wales who built it.

THERE ARE NO FRILLS here: this is a church where the Word is melodiously spoken and sung—and in Welsh (English did not appear at Welsh Hill until 1893).

table for an altar. The emphasis has always been on the Word, and from the beginning, most of the men in the congregation preached the Scriptures.

Welsh Hill is everyman's church, and that is its strength. The Old Welsh Church is like the people who built it: hardworking, modest, and rural. At the height of immigration from Wales in the late nineteenth century, the Welsh had founded well over five hundred churches. Yet, the Welsh never came in great waves, like the Scots and the Irish. Wales might have been as poor as other Celtic regions of the British Isles, but coal meant jobs and less emigration. When they did come, the Welsh tended to settle in rural

THE GRAVESTONES CARRY Welsh names—Edwards, Williams, Jenkins, Jones, Owens—which then became typically American names.

areas, places that reminded them of home and where there was coal to be mined. Although often forgotten, the influence of the Welsh in America was considerable: Welsh names, like those of the pastors here—Jenkins, Edwards, and Williams—became the commonest of American patronymics.

In the early years of North American settlement, dominated by immigrants from Britain, it is not surprising that the Welsh are more than amply represented in halls of power, courts, universities—and not least of all in the antiestablishment sentiments of religious leaders of Welsh descent like Roger

Williams and William Penn (who almost named his colony New Wales). But it was God-fearing miners and no-nonsense farmers in settlements such as Welsh Hill that made northeastern Pennsylvania ring with Celtic echoes (by the end of the nineteenth century Scranton was thirty percent Welsh). Wherever the Welsh went, choir singing went with them (miners from the South Wales town of Merthyr Tydfil reached Salt Lake City, became Mormons, and helped found the Mormon Tabernacle Choir). Bethel Tabernacle still raises its voice in that strong evangelical Protestant tradition.

Saint Cornelia's Episcopal Mission Church,

LOWER SIOUX COMMUNITY, MINNESOTA

*I*t is hardly surprising that many of America's country churches are monuments to missionary fervor. The desire to plant the Cross in a foreign land, to make converts, and later to bring succor to peoples, whose very identity was nearly obliterated by settlement, is particularly poignant when the fusion of Christianity and indigenous religion has been successful. Saint Cornelia's Episcopal Mission Church is a remarkably happy blend of Church of England practice and Dakota Sioux tradition.

Located off County State Aid Highway # 2 in Redwood County, Minnesota, near the Jackpot Junction casino, the church was built by the Dakota congregation. The design, however, is pure Gothic Revival. Cruciform in plan, the granite church has medieval windows filled with stained glass and sloping corner buttresses supporting the nave. The multicolored brick and exposed truss interior could easily pass for a suburban London church by any of the leading nineteenth-century ecclesiastical designers such as William Butterfield, G. E. Street, or their many followers. Nevertheless, certain details, such as the Dakota-inscribed altar and the star quilt behind it—not to mention services—are vivid reminders that Saint Cornelia's is a sacred place for Indians.

The church is also a tribute to two exceptionally fearless white clergymen: Henry Whipple and Samuel Hinman. This was the first of a number of handsome Gothic churches that Bishop Whipple built in Minnesota during his episcopacy, but he is best remembered for his missionary work and for his championship of the Dakota people. The mission was founded as Saint John's in 1860, with Hinman as the priest. Construction on a new church stopped

SAINT CORNELIA'S WAS BUILT by Bishop Henry Whipple, a champion of the Dakota Sioux tribe who, through Whipple's efforts, were brought back to Minnesota from exile in South Dakota.

when the Dakota were dispersed following the Sioux Uprising in 1862. Bishop Whipple interceded with president Lincoln and saved the lives of 269 rebels, but the Dakota (whom the government called Sioux, which was their Ojibwa enemies' derogatory name for them) were dispersed to Nebraska and South Dakota. Father Hinman went into exile with the tribe, while Bishop Whipple lobbied Congress to allow the Dakota to return to their ancestral lands along the Minnesota River.

In 1886, Reverend Hinman and his Dakota wife returned with the Mdewakanton band of Dakotas and began building a new church on land donated by Andrew Good Thunder, the first person Hinman had baptized twenty-five years before. The church is built of local granite, but two distinct colors represent stones from the abandoned church and newly quarried stones. The church was finished in 1889 and was given a new name in honor of the bishop's wife, Cornelia. The rose window over the entrance is a memorial to Mrs. Whipple, while the arched stained-glass window over the altar is dedicated to Father Hinman. Good Thunder and Hinman are buried aside the church.

It is perhaps not un-coincidental that the Sioux Uprising and the enactment of the Homestead Act came about in the same year. The Dakota Sioux had given over most of southern Minnesota in the previous decade. Now they were facing extinction, through crowding out by the settlers and through assimilation. Yet, Saint Cornelia's bridges the time before the Dakota were defeated and sent away and their successful return. Early-twentieth-century photographs show dark-skinned Dakota dressed in the white surplices of the Church of England. Who is to say who has assimilated whom, or which faith is the more flexible, the stronger?

Conanicut Friends Meeting,

JAMESTOWN, RHODE ISLAND

onanicut Friends Meeting, built in Conanicut Island's Jamestown in 1786, is not much larger than a cottage, yet the island was so thoroughly Quaker that no other churches appeared on it until 1830. Nantucket can claim the only other Quaker meeting-house on an island, but Conanicut was quite unlike that whaling port and far different in character from the colonial capital at Newport visible across the harbor. Jamestown was rural, and except for vacation homes along the water, much of the island retains its country character. Until recently, it would be accurate to speak of Jamestown as isolated—the bridge to the mainland opened in 1940, while the span to Newport was not completed for another three decades. Travel to the island was by boat and dependent upon the weather, and so Jamestown retained the feeling of an agricultural outpost. It is said that early explorers noted the resemblance of the Jamestown–Newport Narrows to the ancient harbor at Rhodes (hence the state's name), but the landscape near the meeting-house is open, with hedgerow-framed fields running down to the water—more Irish Sea than Aegean.

THE SOCIETY OF FRIENDS FOUND a welcome in religiously tolerant Rhode Island. Conanicut Meeting replaced one burned by British soldiers during the Revolutionary War.

VIRTUALLY UNCHANGED OVER two hundred years—the meetinghouse has never been electrified and a single wood stove supplies heat, yet Conanicut maintains the eloquence of silence.

Conanicut Friends Meeting is a simple box, sheathed with prototypical yet humble wooden shakes. The meetinghouse has never been electrified; a wood stove provides heat, and a divider can be dropped down to concentrate worshipers in the side with the stove. Philadelphians who summer on the island have financed some partial restoration, but otherwise the building has endured in its simplicity for more than two centuries. Yet, no one who attended a First Day gathering at Conanicut would suggest that the plain benches, the roughly plastered walls, the faded teal paint of the framing members, and the light through ancient wavy yet clear glass are any less eloquent a reflection of God's word than colored windows or carved masonry.

THE EIGHTEENTH-CENTURY WINDMILL is another reminder of the very rural nature of Conanicut Island.

Holy Trinity Temple,

WILKESON, WASHINGTON

Holy Trinity Temple challenges a lot of our perceptions about the settlement of the American West. As a Russian Orthodox church it also makes us look a little differently at the religious development of the frontier.

The blue onion dome with its three-bar Slavic cross makes it clear that Congregationalist New Englanders traveling the Oregon Trail did not build this Washington variant of the simple white frame church. Nor was it erected by the Spanish friars who Christianized the Southwest. Rather, the second oldest Orthodox church south of Alaska was the result of colonization from that Russian imperial outpost. Although a Muscovite bishop consecrated it, it was established to serve a polyglot group of miners from various outposts of Eastern Orthodoxy.

It is perhaps easy to forget the important role of coal mining in opening the trans-Mississippi half of the country, just as we sometimes forget the different ethnic and religious groups that followed the cattlemen and homesteaders. The railroads were fueled by coal, deposits of which were found in the Carbon River valley near Mount Rainier in the 1860s. The Northern Pacific Railroad constructed a line from the coalfields to Tacoma to supply its trains, but this particular coal was discovered to make good coke. So, the Tacoma Coal and Coke Company built the first coke oven in Wilkeson (named for a Northern Pacific geological surveyor) in 1885, and soon there were more than a hundred ovens and several thousand people in this booming town.

The immigrant culture we might associate with New York was certainly found in Wilkeson (although Chinese were excluded). Most of the miners were Slovaks from the Carpathian Mountains, although

EXCEPT FOR THE SLAVIC CROSS, this could be another example of the standard white preaching box, yet Holy Trinity was built by Slovak, Russian, Turkish, and even Arab miners in this coal mining region of the Pacific Northwest.

the original forty-two-person congregation at Holy Trinity included Russians, Greeks, and Arabs, as well as Slavs. The miners helped construct the church and donated the icons and furnishings.

Bishop Tikhon consecrated Holy Trinity in 1902. As the Enlightener of North America, Tikhon established a seminary in Minneapolis, a monastery in Pennsylvania, and the cathedral in New York. He believed that the Orthodox Church in America should be self-governing (a status it achieved in 1970) and multiethnic. In 1917, Tikhon was called back to a Russia in turmoil, where he was elected Patriarch of the Russian Orthodox Church. Imprisoned and tortured by the Soviets, Tikhon was glorified as a saint.

The temple looks very much as it did during Tikhon's visit, although it now has a new icon of Saint Tikhon holding Holy Trinity in his hands. Thanks to a couple who kept the church going after the mines closed, the Orthodox sanctuary is still used for weddings, funerals, Theophany (January 6), and the annual blessing of the waters. The wooden screen—iconostasis—still separates the laity from the priest, and its wooden panels still carry the icons of Jesus and Mary painted in the realistic Carpatho-Ukrainian style. From the outside, Holy Trinity Temple may look not unlike so many of its American brethren. But inside, with its brightly painted images, brass chandelier, and numerous candles, the spirit is very much eastern European.

Rockingham Meeting House,

ROCKINGHAM, VERMONT

Rockingham Meeting House is situated atop a hill overlooking a river valley. It remains at the geographic center of Rockingham, but the town's population has long since moved from upland farms to industrial settlements in Bellows Falls, Saxtons River, and the world beyond. The idyllic setting is prototypical Vermont, while the cubic white meetinghouse is one of the handsomest and best-preserved examples of its type.

From the arrival of the Pilgrims and Puritans, the New England meetinghouse was both church and town hall—ironically theocratic but eminently practical. The earliest meetinghouses were often square, somewhat ungainly boxes reminiscent of English barns, but by the time coastal New Englanders were settling Vermont, the meetinghouse had evolved into a more geometric and formal configuration (Rockingham's dimensions are forty-four by fifty-six feet, and forty-four feet tall). Rockingham is one of the very last examples of this second phase of the New England meetinghouse, as the shape had long since evolved into the more characteristic church with a steeple over the entrance on the narrow end, instead of in the middle of the long side, as here.

Rockingham is built like a barn, and the formality of its facade actually reflects its internal post-and-beam construction. But there is nothing medieval or even backcounty in its lavish door treatment. It seems as if the entire decorative energy was spent on the building's entrance. The details were no doubt found in a builder's handbook that allowed rural carpenters to ape the manner of Philadelphia and London, but here the local housewright created the perfect balance of light and shadow with pediment and pilasters, modillion cornice and entablature, in an overall

ROCKINGHAM MEETING HOUSE was abandoned around 1870 and not restored until 1906, but the cemetery has served the town from the 1770s to the present.

BUILT LIKE A BARN—sturdy and functional—the Rockingham Meeting is a large preaching hall that was also used for town meetings at which the entire population could be accommodated.

composition of impeccable sophistication.

The same holds true of the interior where the main focus is the pulpit opposite the entrance. There are ample box pews, and a second-story gallery that runs three-quarters around the room, not to mention vertical framing posts. But it is the pulpit—nine feet from the floor, lighted by a large round-arched window, and topped with a giant polygonal sounding board—that grabs one's attention. Except for the pulpit and the turned pulpit-railing spindles, this preaching space is plain—there is no glass or color or finery to detract from the minister's sermon.

As the town's second meetinghouse, Rockingham was begun in 1787, completed in 1801, and served as the town church until 1838; the last town meeting was held here in 1869. Abandoned and vandalized, the church was restored in 1906; the pulpit, which had been lowered in 1851, was the only conjectural part

of a restoration notable for being both early and sensitive.

If you really want to read the history of the town, and of Vermont itself, wander the cemetery. Here are a thousand headstones, marking burials from earlier than the meetinghouse until the present. These include naive but powerful early carvings in slate, of sunbursts, angels, urns, willow trees, and death's-heads by a handful of different stonecutters. And there are the all-too-poignant stones, whether slate, Victorian figures, or contemporary polished marble noting too-soon-departed children. A seraph's head flies above the inscription: "In Memory of William Warren, Son of mr. David and mrs. Salley Oakes who died June 6th, 1802: aged 6 years, one month, and thirteen Days." A praying Virgin Mary memorializes a seventeen-year-old son who died in 1974, two centuries after the founding of the meetinghouse.

Saint Andrew's Church,

PRAIRIEVILLE, ALABAMA

There is a melancholy to Saint Andrew's Church that is palpable. The wooden church with its cemetery of weathered stones, outlined by a wrought-iron fence, seems to evoke sadness for times lost. Antebellum clichés notwithstanding, this Episcopal church symbolizes the richness of Alabama's eponymous Black Belt, where the fertile soil was worked by slaves on large plantations. Once the literal heart of Dixie (only a few miles from Selma and the civil rights marches of the 1960s), time appears to have passed by this part of the rural South. Parishioners have scattered, and the church is open only for special services to bless the animals and crops. Yet this house of worship is a gem, treasured and maintained as such.

Saint Andrew's was the first of a series of wooden Gothic Revival churches built for Episcopalians in the Canebreak, an area settled by planters from the Atlantic seaboard, who referred to the flat farmland as the prairie. The Reverend Caleb Ives, who subsequently established several parishes in plantation country, first held services in here in 1834. The church itself was built by slave labor in 1852–53, with Peter Lee and Joe Glasgow serving as the master carpenters. The intricate iron hinges on the entrance door were wrought in the plantation forge, while the interior walls were colored with a tobacco-based stain.

Despite the use of bonded manpower in an isolated frontier locale, Saint Andrew's represented up-to-date church design. The Gothic style was very popular in the pre–Civil War South: pointed-arch windows and medieval verticality reflected the vogue for the novels of Sir Walter Scott, English Romantic poetry, and even notions of chivalry. Saint Andrew's is in fact attributed to Richard Upjohn, the nineteenth century's leading ecclesiastical architect and the designer of the

CARPENTERS FROM NEARBY plantations built this Rural Gothic church, probably to plans provided by leading ecclesiastical architect Richard Upjohn. Such sophistication speaks of the agricultural wealth of this region of Alabama before the Civil War.

THE EASTLAKE STYLE Mason & Hamlin pump organ replaced the earlier harmonium with its appropriately castellated Gothic case. The deep chancel was a hallmark of Upjohn's Episcopal churches.

archetypal Gothic Revival church, Trinity in New York.

The English-born Upjohn became so popular that he could not keep up with the demand (he would design for other denominations, but he reserved the Gothic style solely for Episcopalians). Even though he donated his services to one parish a year, he met some of the clamor for his talents, particularly among poorer congregations, by publishing a how-to guide called *Upjohn's Rural Architecture*. The book offered diagrams of plans (long and narrow), window configurations (pointed), and other details (buttresses and a plain bell tower) so that a new church could look reasonably correct—an English parish church

re-created in board-and-batten at very low cost.

Saint Andrew's undoubtedly had a tower that has not survived (it was apparently a particular favorite with woodpeckers), but otherwise the church stands as it was built.

Whether the Prairieville church was based on Upjohn's book or on plans the architect sent to Alabama, it is fair to call this and the subsequent nearby ones Upjohn churches. Saint Andrew's Church was certainly a model to be emulated across rural America. And it showed, too—as so many of these country churches do—that distance from civilization was not a proper measure of sophistication and aspiration.

STAINED WITH TOBACCO, the pews look like simple tombstones,
while the monuments in the church cemetery are far more elaborate.

Phippsburg Congregational Church,
PHIPPSBURG, MAINE

*I*n 1774, an Irishman named James McCobb, a captain in the First Lincoln County Regiment of Colonial Militia, planted a linden tree on a rise overlooking the Kennebec River. Twenty-five years later, his widow, Mary, donated land next to the tree for the building of a Congregational church. Today, the linden is Maine's largest and, at about a hundred feet, rivals the church steeple.

Both tree and church are landmarks along an historically eventful stretch of river. Benedict Arnold passed through here on his ill-fated expedition to Quebec. Phippsburg was a major shipbuilding town, and during the War of 1812, the naval battle between the H.M.S. *Boxer* and the American ship *Enterprise* was so close offshore that residents could hear the cannons. A few miles south of the church, where the Kennebec meets the sea, English colonists had settled in 1607 and built an Anglican chapel; although contemporaneous with Jamestown, the settlement was abandoned soon thereafter.

There was not a church in Phippsburg until 1734, when Scots Presbyterians erected a meetinghouse. In 1765, a handful of members withdrew and built their own Congregational church on Arrowsic Island. While an island church was safer from Indian attacks, it was rather inconvenient, especially in winter. So the island meetinghouse was torn down and the present church built, completed in 1802.

The thirty-nine- by sixty-one-foot church was the center of a bustling community, serving as town hall until church and state were officially separated in Maine in 1822. Warships are still built upriver at Bath; nineteenth-century Phippsburg was an equally important launching place for wooden ships in the golden age of sail.

Shipbuilding made Phippsburg relatively wealthy,

THE TALLEST LINDEN in the Pine Tree State shades the grave of Maine's first congressman and competes with the Gothic-over-Greek steeple of the Congregational Church. The church is a landmark along the Kennebec, a river steeped in early American history.

IN 1952, 150 YEARS AFTER the church's founding, electricity was installed and the interior was
redecorated, adding new carpets, pew cushions, hymn books, and new upholstering to the pulpit chairs.

and in 1846 the Congregationalists totally "new modeled" the church. Except for the replacement of the
twenty-over-twenty clear windows with stained glass
in 1909, the church looks now as it did then. Maine
in the 1840s was enthralled by both the Greek and
Gothic Revivals, and Phippsburg is a little of each.
The roof was lowered slightly, and columnlike corner
pilasters accentuated the building's natural temple
form. Perhaps not as refined as an ancient Greek

temple, the entablature across the main facade comprises three lapped boards that are 7 ¾, 11 ¾, and
16 ⅝ inches wide, respectively.

The first steeple was blown off in the 1820s, and
its replacement is a variation on the basic New
England type that had been around since the 1770s.
But here the two-tier bell tower and spire have wood-
en obelisks at each corner that give the ensemble a
more medieval touch. The most delightful Gothic

PHIPPSBURG IS ONE OF the oldest settlements in North America, but its boom was during the days of building wooden ships. Despite the wealth that allowed the updating of the church in the 1840s, the interior is no-nonsense Congregationalist preaching box. The white church functions like a lighthouse for this part of the river: *A light shines in the darkness and the darkness has not overcome it* (John 1:5).

feature is the treatment of the flanking entrance doors: the plain pilasters of the frames bend together, until their tips form a crown reminiscent of a fleur-de-lis or a poppy. To call this Carpenters Gothic implies a naïveté, or at least the limitations of wood-working tools in the 1840s, but who can doubt that this small sensual flourish was intentional.

The local shipbuilding that made the renovations possible in 1846 declined as the century wore on. The church was closed for long periods, often open only for summer services; electricity was installed in 1952,

a furnace in 1967. But this was a blessing, for aside from the new windows and the occasional coat of paint, the church looks pretty much as it always has.

But it is the eighty-foot steeple that remains the landmark, a beacon visible from the river and lighted at night. Phippsburg is a classic symbol of the country church, or as the present organist notes: "This tall building is the physical remnant of the faith our ancestors had in God." One member of the congregation for over fifty years says it best: "It's been a landmark all my life . . . to me it means home."

PROJECT ORIGINATOR AND EDITOR: Richard Olsen
DESIGNERS: Michael J. Walsh Jr., Christine Knorr, Arlene Lee
PRODUCTION MANAGER: Jane G. Searle
EDITORIAL ASSISTANT: Sigi Nacson

Library of Congress Cataloging-in-Publication Data

Morgan, William, 1944-
  American country churches / by William Morgan ; principal
  photography
  by Radek Kurzaj.
    p. cm.
  Includes index.
  ISBN 0-8109-4335-2 (alk. paper)
  1. Rural churches—United States—Pictorial works. 2. Church
  architecture—United States—Pictorial works. I. Kurzaj, Radek, 1976–
  II. Title.

  NA5205.M67 2004
  726.5'0973'091734—dc22

          2003021466

Text copyright © 2004 William Morgan
All photographs copyright © 2004 Radek Kurzaj, except those
appearing on: 11; 12–13; 52; 53; 54; 55; 56; 57; 96; 97; 98; 99; 100; 100–101; 132;
133; 134; 135; 136–137; 137; 187; 188; 189; 190–191; 191; 210–211; 212; 212–213;
214–215; 222; 223; 224; 225; 232; 233; 234; 235; 236; and 237.

Copyright © 2004 William Morgan.

Published in 2004 by Harry N. Abrams, Incorporated, New York

Printed and bound in China
10 9 8 7 6 5 4 3 2

Harry N. Abrams, Inc.
100 Fifth Avenue
New York, NY 10011
www.abramsbooks.com

ABRAMS IS A SUBSIDIARY OF LA MARTINIÈRE GROUPE